NO MATTER HOW ... YOU *CAN* HELP YOUR CHILD TO MAKE THE GRADE!

"EVERY PARENT WILL FIND MEANINGFUL AP-PLICATIONS—*Boosting the Underachiever* could very well have been entitled *Everything You Need to Know About Educating Your Child*. In a non-jargonized, very readable book, Dr. Cogen focuses on the child who is learning significantly below his or her potential . . . a wise book obviously written by a ripe, insightful educator."
>   —I. RALPH HYATT, Ed.D., Professor Emeritus of Psychology, St. Joseph's University

"*Boosting the Underachiever* is a thoughtful volume, readable and practical for parents and teachers. It should have a wide appeal, as it contains good suggestions for parents without making unreasonable demands of them."
>   —IRVING E. SIGEL, Distinguished Research Scientist, Educational Testing Service (Creators of the Scholastic Aptitude Test, or SAT)

"IF THERE IS ANY SINGLE MESSAGE THAT STANDS OUT, IT IS THAT EACH CHILD IS A UNIQUE INDIVIDUAL . . . Cogen assumes that many, if not most, parents are very good at worrying. Following his advice can serve to alleviate much of that anxiousness about their children."
>   —*USA TODAY*

BOOSTING THE UNDERACHIEVER

How Busy Parents Can Unlock Their Child's Potential

VICTOR COGEN, Ed.D.

BERKLEY BOOKS, NEW YORK

BOOSTING THE UNDERACHIEVER

A Berkley Book / published by arrangement with
Plenum Publishing Corporation

PRINTING HISTORY
Plenum edition published 1990
Berkley edition / May 1992

ISBN: 0-425-13272-2

A BERKLEY BOOK ® TM 757,375
Berkley Books are published by The Berkley Publishing Group,
200 Madison Avenue, New York, New York 10016.
The name "BERKLEY" and the "B" logo
are trademarks belonging to Berkley Publishing Corporation.

PRINTED IN THE UNITED STATES OF AMERICA

10 9 8 7 6 5 4 3 2 1

PREFACE

In 1969, I accepted an invitation to join a series of conferences to explore the possibility of applying the theories of Jean Piaget to the teaching of young children with severe learning difficulties. Piaget, who has since passed away, still stands as a giant in the field of child development.

A basic team of educators and psychologists was organized under the project director, Dr. Mortimer Garrison, Jr., to participate in each session, held in the Woods Schools in Langhorne, Pennsylvania. In addition to Garrison and myself, the team included Irving E. Sigel, Chairman of Research at the Merrill-Palmer Institute, Will Beth Stephens, recently from Illinois Cognitive Studies, and Harold A. Delp, Special Education Department Head at Temple University.

A prominent guest was invited to attend each of these federally funded meetings. These scholars included Donald S. Baer, Department of Human Development, University of Kansas; Joachim F. Wohlwill, Department of Psychology, Clark University; Thomas J. Banta, Department of Psychology, University of Cincinnati; and Frances P. Conner, Head of Special Education, Teachers College, Columbia University.

The participants represented quite diverse schools of thought but were able to engage in objective and in-depth analyses of each suggestion. I came away from that project impressed by the contribution each scholar had made to answering the question of how children learn.

This contact clarified an evolving notion that I had become more than a learning or curriculum specialist. My task, I decided, was to bridge the gap between the various branches of psychology and education. I could no longer consider myself a "behaviorist" or "cognitive theorist" or even a "programmatic specialist." Instead, I had to become an "eclectical pragmatist." In other words, if a proposition worked, I used it. For almost 20 years, I followed that strategy. This book is the result of my direct experience with what works.

I am grateful to the many teachers who have shed light on how children learn, and to the parents who reported the results of trying out aspects of the program. I'm indebted to Linda Greenspan Regan, senior editor, her assistant, Naomi Brier, and copyeditor May Dikeman, who cleared the manuscript of grammatical weeds while insisting upon precision and clarity. Finally, I dedicate this work to my most uncompromising critic, Betty Mosley Cogen, my wife, who always rejected "good enough" as not being good enough.

CONTENTS

vii

PART III
THE REMEDIAL PROCESS

PROLOGUE

Franklin's "Stitch"

Some years ago, a teacher enrolled in one of my graduate classes asked, "What should I have done when a student threw a board eraser at me?"

"It shouldn't have happened," I shot back.

At first the members of the class thought I was simply using my position to avoid a difficult question. But in the ensuing discussion and analysis most realized that the incident couldn't be examined objectively in isolation. It had to be the last link in a chain of causes. The escalating problem should have been identified and attended to long before the board eraser became a missile.

A teacher should not be the target of a youngster's anger. However, such an act is indicative of something much deeper—a disquieting frustration in the child. This is one example of how a problem might fester, affecting not only learning but stability.

A child's failure to function at a reasonable level is the prime concern of this work. The sooner his or her problems are recognized and addressed, the easier the process of recovery will be. You should not wait. Timely action may well prevent you from facing a school authority someday who will tell you, "It shouldn't have happened."

INTRODUCTION

Though more underachievers pervade the school system than all of the special education students combined, there are virtually no special services available to help them.

Programs abound for children with various handicaps, for gifted youngsters, and for talented students, such as those with musical ability. All of these programs are useful and most rate highly on a success chart. Funding is also available for programs under the label of compensatory education, for the environmentally disadvantaged. But since underachievers do not usually cause disciplinary problems or attract attention to themselves in other ways, they are often overlooked.

"Underachieving" is a rather nebulous term. In this book, I define underachievers as normal children whose academic performance is *significantly* below their potential. These children are not hampered by an impairment or an inner-city disadvantage. They do not necessarily fail, but they do earn grades below reasonable expectations. For instance, children who could be receiving A's or B's may be satisfied with C's or even D's. Children who should excel are barely scraping by.

These children, who do not perform close to their abilities, tend to slip through the cracks of the educational floor. However, there is a solution. If your child is an underachiever, with some effort and knowledge you can do something about it.

Schools Under Fire

It is as predictable as the morning school bell. Every few years a prominent person or appointed commission comes forward with a warning about the regrettable state of America's schools. The educational system, they note, is failing to produce enough literate and skilled graduates to meet modern domestic requirements and current global competition. A prime example is the 1983 federally supported report "A Nation at Risk: The Imperative for Education Reform," which summed up its findings by describing the current system as "producing a rising tide of mediocrity."

In another case a former Secretary of Education, William Bennett, known for expressing his opinions candidly, rated America's schools at C to C+. *The Wall Street Journal,* in its 36-page analysis, on March 31, 1989, succinctly stated the widespread feeling of the public: "The system needs a complete overhaul, and not just more tinkering." In May of 1989, Secretary of Education Lauro Cavazos noted that progress was stagnant. Ironically, the school system itself, by these evaluations, could aptly be described as an underachiever.

Despite election promises by political candidates, the public schools face overwhelming problems and are not likely to change dramatically in the near future. Although many children succeed in our current school system, many do not. If your child is one of them and is not doing as well as he or she should, you can't afford to wait for possible future improvements in education. You must take on the role of promoting the academic development of your child *now.*

Finding Help

Few parents are qualified and/or inclined to teach their children at home. Fewer still can afford to employ full-time tutors. Therefore, most parents of underachievers must seek other alternatives.

Private schools are not always convenient, not always better, but always high-priced. Learning centers address specific failures rather than broad underperformance. In addition, each *hour* of instruction in a tutoring organization costs as much as a broad-based book on the topic.

Another choice remains, the most effective and least expensive one: the public elementary school and *you*—an interested and knowledgeable parent. By supporting the school and following a prescribed program for your child, as set out in the following chapters, you can make a difference in your child's academic achievement. The plan is specifically designed for busy parents of children in kindergarten through sixth grade.

The Program

Acting now will enable you to provide a learning-assistance program which supplements, not supplants, the efforts of the school. You will be able to take full advantage of the existing educational system while your child masters the fundamentals of learning.

The distinguished author Leslie M. LeCron observed: "It is truly amazing and also ridiculous that in our educational system there is almost never any attempt made to teach students how to study efficiently, or how to take and prepare for examinations." Your goal, after arming yourself with the present material, is to change the consequences of this omission.

All of the procedures I'll cover are suitable for use by parents and will take into account the time constraints of single, career, and very busy parents. The reader is not expected to have unlimited resources. Furthermore, no special materials or equipment are required and your child will not need a tutor.

The first section of the book enables you to determine if your youngster is a true underachiever. The second section describes the causes of underachievement. Parental and sometimes professional explanations that "He just doesn't try," or is "lazy" are, with few exceptions, inadequate. *Why* doesn't he try, and, if he's lazy, *why* is that so? Children, by nature, are inquisitive and active. By matching your child against classic underachievers, you will gain considerable insight into the situation and learn the steps that can help bring about improvement.

The third section—the major portion and the essence of this

work—includes both general and specific recommendations on how to weed out the underlying causes of the problem rather than simply provide symptomatic relief.

Central to the advancement of children is the theme "learning to learn." The multitude of components necessary for this process cannot be enumerated, but particular attention is paid to certain basic points. Children will learn how to:

- Start an assignment
- Gauge their own progress
- Find assistance when needed
- Check and evaluate results

- Become self-starters
- Utilize their own resources
- Employ past experiences on new problems
- Develop self-reliance
- Become efficient

- Use their own learning styles
- Avoid pitfalls
- Work with others
- Work alone
- Reinforce what they've learned
- Overcome fears of failure
- Listen intently

- Study for tests
- Rebound from setbacks
- Think critically
- Anticipate later requirements
- Adjust to a classroom environment
- Delay gratification
- Overcome frustration
- Become achievers

Teachers recognize the importance of individual differences in children but can do little to accommodate them—you can. By utilizing your child's unique attributes and learning style, you can help him reach his appropriate state of learning readiness. Psychologists are aware of the importance of readiness. A youngster cannot learn adequately until his cognitive, emotional, and social components are at the necessary level. The recommended procedures, bolstering natural drives, will raise your child to this required state.

Every recommendation can be carried out by the typical parent, regardless of other obligations. An honest effort on your part will propel your child toward his optimal level.

Please read all of the sections, including those that may not appear applicable at present. All of the content is given for a reason. As Chekhov pointed out about writing, if a firearm appears in the first act, it should go off before the end of the play. All of the elements in this book follow that philosophy. They're all part of the program and will eventually be used.

A Technicality

To avoid the stilted "his or her," where gender is not specifically identified, I refer to the parent as a mother and the child as a son throughout the rest of the text. I also refer to a teacher as "she." The linguists, who produced the satisfactory "Ms." to fill a need, seem to be very slow in finding a substitute for the awkward his/her.

Observations

Some researchers will find much of the material presented here worthy of future investigation. A few educators will consider any departure from conventional approaches to be questionable and controversial. But, consider this: If educators have an effective prescription, why is your child an underachiever?

Finally, be aware that requirements exist for carrying out the suggestions successfully. You must have a great love for your child; you must be willing to spend a few hours with him each week; and you must possess at least a minimal sense of humor. If you cannot answer affirmatively to each precondition, put the book back on the shelf.

Most underachieving children can be helped dramatically. Here you will learn the skills to help your child.

PART I

IS YOUR CHILD AN UNDERACHIEVER?

1

The Profile
Do You Recognize
This Behavior?

Is This You?

A group of mothers squirm uncomfortably in the child-sized seats waiting to converse one-on-one with the teacher. Periodically, the school, wishing to involve parents in the education of its youngsters, makes this opportunity available. Some parents attend each conference; some come occasionally; some never come at all.

Mrs. Bennett's attention is attracted to a display board listing the students alphabetically. Vertical columns represent the various subjects, and gold stars in these columns triumphantly proclaim a student's success. Most of the pupils have earned multiple stars. Mrs. Bennett's son, Josh, has only one. Just as she is beginning to ponder the significance of this observation, the teacher nods at her. Mrs. Bennett gladly exchanges the uncomfortable child's seat for the adult chair next to the teacher. She wishes, however, that there were some way to postpone hearing the disheartening news about her child.

"Miss Leady, I'm Josh's mother. I understand he isn't doing well."

"Well, yes, that's right, Mrs. Bennett. Josh's test scores

are among the lowest in the class. This comparison chart shows that his grades fall below most of the other children in our studies.''

''He's high over there,'' notes Josh's mother, pointing at the wall chart.

''Yes. He's quite good in physical education and that's important, but he trails in subjects that require more concentration.''

''Are you saying Josh is dumb?''

''No, of course not. Mrs. Bennett, Josh is anything but slow. His IQ is above average. The fact that he doesn't do well in some subjects doesn't mean that he isn't capable of better work.''

''Why doesn't he do well?'' asks the mother, hoping her son's problem can be corrected easily.

''That's difficult to say. He's just not motivated; at least, not enough.''

''Why isn't he motivated? Isn't it the school's job to motivate children?''

''Yes, it is, and we try. That's what teaching is all about. We use a variety of techniques to . . .''

''But they don't work.''

''They work for most of the children. But sometimes a child just does not respond well. His learning is simply not commensurate with his ability.''

''You mean he's learning-disabled?''

''No, Mrs. Bennett. Learning-disabled children have some kind of neurological interference. They have what we call 'minimal cerebral dysfunction.' ''

''They have something wrong with their brains?''

''No. Not exactly. The cause can't be specifically diagnosed.''

''But Josh isn't learning-disabled?''

''No. Josh simply is an underachiever.''

''What happens now? Will he be put into a special class?''

''No, Mrs. Bennett. There is no special class for students like Josh.''

''Doesn't this district have special classes?''

''We have special classes, Mrs. Bennett. We have programs for the retarded, visually or hearing-impaired, emotionally disturbed and, of course, the learning-disabled.''

"But Josh . . ."

"Josh is normal, Mrs. Bennett. His only difficulty is one of adjustment to school.''

Many parents find themselves in Mrs. Bennett's position. They expect to hear that their child is "not living up to his potential," but hope that the teacher, with her training and experience, will offer a solution. Instead, they learn that the teacher isn't overly concerned because, after all, "Josh is simply an underachiever." Though there are many students in this predicament, it somehow isn't very comforting to the parent.

If you, like Mrs. Bennett, have been informed that your child's IQ is above average while his performance is below the norm, you would want an explanation. If the cause of poor work is not a lack in his innate capacity, then his environment must be at fault. But is it really? You have given him a good home. You express your love with actions and words. You are interested in his behavior, his thoughts and feelings. You're not an expert on child development and you make mistakes, but you're a good parent. Even though you are often busy, you make time for your child—quality time.

Still, you haven't been oblivious to the unfolding events. You have discussed school with him many times. You have tried encouragement, reasoning, rewards. You have been patient, sometimes exercising great restraint. You might even have tried punishment. Yet all of your efforts seem to be in vain. He doesn't share your worry about his future. He promises to improve, or claims he is trying. Sometimes he even patronizes *you*.

Underachievement is exasperating because you understand the necessity of a good education in this competitive world. You want your child to make optimal use of his native resources, and you feel that the current period of his life is critical. He should be constructing a firm foundation for future growth. You feel a bone-penetrating chill when you contemplate the possibility of your child becoming a loser. But how do you get him to do his best? How do you make your bright child shine?

Don't Duck the Duck Test

Your initial task is to determine whether your child is really an underachiever. You can do this by administering the duck test. If it looks, walks, and quacks like a duck, it's a duck.

If he (1) *behaves* like an underachiever; (2) *performs* like an underachiever; and (3) has *ability* above his performance level, then your child is an underachiever.

Behavior

A child's behavior offers clues to his attitudes and way of thinking. Children tend to express themselves through actions instead of words. But most children, at some time, will act like an underachiever. No one incident is sufficient to categorize a child. You should look for a pattern of behavior.

Many children do not like school, but the typical underachiever makes not going to school his cause. He never exhausts his reasons for staying home. Carl, a spunky, intelligent child, started in first grade to find excuses for avoiding school. He has since built a repertoire of justifications for remaining at home:

"Mom, I have this pain in my stomach."

"I can't go to school today. I forgot to do my homework."

"No sense in going to school. My teacher won't be in the whole week, so we'll just have a sub and we won't learn anything."

"I'm not ready for the big test so I'll just fail it. But if I stay home I can study and take a makeup later."

"Dad took a day off. Why can't I? I need a break too."

"Look at that rain. I'm sure I'll get sick if I go out."

Sometimes, instead of excuses for avoiding school, he demonstrates defiance or ambivalence:

"No. I'm not going. Never."

"No. Not today. Maybe I'll go tomorrow."

Many children use school-evasion tactics similar to Carl's and offer unsolicited criticisms of the school:

"You don't learn anything."
"It's so boring."
"It's a waste of time."
"School stinks."

As Carl grows older, he develops more sophisticated school-avoidance techniques. Although his mother is familiar with every ploy, other adults are not. For example, one morning the child claims he is not well. His mother finds nothing wrong and sends him to school. Later the school nurse telephones to say Carl needs medical treatment. He has, in fact, convinced the nurse he is sick. The determined boy has become accomplished in simulating an upset stomach, and, on occasion, can even induce a bout of diarrhea.

Another time, the school secretary calls for confirmation. Carl is requesting an early dismissal in order to attend his grandfather's funeral. His grandfather and several aunts and uncles have conveniently "died" many times before.

The situation continues to deteriorate. One spring morning, after being awakened and forced to dress, Carl announces he is not attending school that day. His mother skirts the usual arguments but, aware of his determination, drives him to school. She watches him enter the building before driving away, not knowing Carl is leaving by a back door.

Sara, like Carl, has developed a negative attitude toward formal learning. Although she finds going to school tolerable, if only barely, she has trouble with particular subjects. "Why must they teach us arithmetic? I can count. Who needs all those fractions? The whole thing is so stupid."

Nine-year-old Sara achieves success in some subjects but consistently underperforms in others. She is capable of doing well in arithmetic but is turned off in this area.

Carl, now in third grade, represents the group that generally does poorly across the spectrum, but does, on occasion, rise to considerable academic heights: "Mom, guess what? The teacher said my science project was the best in the class."

When motivated, Carl's work reflects his true ability, but he tends to leave his parents frustrated when, as his interest fades, his grades decline. While they exhibit somewhat different profiles, both Sara and Carl are underachievers.

For the most part, underachievers adjust to school by carefully measuring their efforts to avoid doing more than the minimum. This subconscious plan of action usually results in careless, disorganized work. For instance, homework is a chore to "put behind you"—fast. Their halfhearted efforts are accompanied by remarks such as:

"That's the best I can do."
"It's here somewhere. I'll find it tomorrow."
"I'm through. That's all anybody does."
"The teacher doesn't expect any more than that."

Children such as Sara and Carl are easily thwarted. They want assignments to be routine and problems to be easily solved.

"I tried. I just can't do it."
"There's no way to finish this."

Postponement is often an escape mechanism.

"I'll do it later."
"There's plenty of time in the morning."
"I can do it in school."

If Sara's parents insist on assignments being completed, she unveils her litany of work-evading excuses:

"I can't do it now. Mary talked to me when the teacher explained it and I didn't hear her."
"The teacher forgot to tell us how to do it."
"I was absent when they went over that."
"I lost the directions."

Unsatisfactory consequences of below-par efforts are explained away:

"It's not important. I don't have to know that stuff."

"So I won't go to college. So what?"

"That *is* my best. Can I play my tape now?"

In general, underachieving children are satisfied to coast through school:

"I'm doing fine," said the fifth-grader. "I passed everything and even got a C+ and a B−."

"Not everybody is an 'A' student. I don't need good grades."

Lack of interest and unsatisfactory progress in school does not necessarily mean that the children have shut themselves off to the world. They may have a variety of other interests or they may become engrossed in one main nonacademic activity.

Nine-year-old Ralph: "Skating is great. Watch what I can do."

Seven-year-old Sean: "That's a Buick Century. And that blue one is an Eldorado. Wow! And, look at that new eight-cylinder Lincoln."

Eleven-year-old Maureen: "Yes. Yes. Then right after the soccer game we're going to Suzanne's and order pizza and have a slumber party."

All children are unique, but if your child demonstrates behavior similar to that described above you should continue with the analysis. You now need the other segments of the duck test, the measure of your child's academic performance, and the determination of his natural ability. Since the IQ impacts on the thinking of most people and even affects grades, I shall consider these numbers in the next two chapters. The measure of your child's academic performance will follow in Chapter 4 where you will see that grades may not be as informative as you assume. Remember that marks are based on tests coupled with the subjective judgment of the teacher.

Grades and IQ tests may be evidence enough for schools to categorize children. You, as a parent, must take a broader and more analytical look. In the balance of Part I, I will make this an easy and enlightening task.

2

By the Numbers

The Influencing Agent

The teacher smiled at her class of sixth-graders as she flipped open her roll book containing each pupil's name listed alphabetically. After each name, she had entered the child's IQ. Not yet familiar with the students, she also prepared a large white seating chart with each name in bold green letters.

"Class, we had an introductory assignment yesterday from our textbooks. I hope you found it interesting. Now let's review the material and see what it means." The teacher's eyes darted to the seating chart and came to rest on the name, Fred Walters, row four, seat two.

"Fred, would you tell us, please, the point Stinson Jackson, the author, was making in the first section?"

In row four, seat two, a male student sat impassively. A lengthy five seconds of silence followed. Again, she checked her seating chart. With absolute confidence, the chart indicated that she was correct.

"Are you Fred Walters?" she asked hesitantly. Row four, seat two nodded affirmatively.

"Would you stand up, please?" she requested, suppressing the annoyance creeping into her voice.

"I didn't know for sure you meant me," the boy answered as he rose. "I thought you might mean Fred Collins." He pointed limply to the youngster in front of him.

Eyes to the seating chart. Damn! Fred Collins is in row four, seat one. The two children with the same first name should have been separated.

"That's all right," she acknowledged condescendingly. Let the class know it was his error, not hers. "Now, please explain Mr. Jackson's position in the first segment of your assignment."

Fred showed signs of confusion. He grappled in vain with the elusive concept. He stammered, then fidgeted, and by his gestures appealed for help.

Eyes, this time, to the roll book. Fred Walters, IQ 96. Low normal range. Can't expect too much. Should do passing work with some effort.

Teacher to the rescue. "Fred, I know it is somewhat difficult to understand the author's thinking and you have made a good try. Let's see if someone else can help." Duty done. Fred's feelings are assuaged (presumably). I didn't put the student down. I gave him an out and encouraged him to greater efforts later.—Let's see. That nice looking girl in the rose-colored blouse looks alert.

The seating chart identified her as Joan.

"Joan, would you please comment on Mr. Jackson's position?"

Joan stood up and she, too, showed signs of confusion.

The teacher's eyes went to the roll book again. Joan Cary, IQ 121. Well above average. Superior level. Can do most academic work.

"Joan, now just a minute. Let's take this a step at a time. Does Mr. Jackson have a particular view? Yes? Good. Now, did he favor the movement toward trade unions? He did? Fine! Did he think the movement made a significant contribution to workable labor-management relations? He did? Excellent! Does he feel that labor and industry should now update their relationship? He does? That's right. Good work, Joan. All right, let's go on from there.

"Oh, Fred. You did nicely too."

The teacher in this story was so influenced by IQ scores that she assumed Fred could not follow the author's line of reasoning. On the other hand she assumed that Joan was better equipped to explain the writer's argument. The teacher's expectations for each child's contributions were solely based on IQ scores. She was impatient with Fred who was struggling and obviously needed help. Noting his IQ, she automatically assumed the question she posed was beyond his mental reach. She felt she had erred in calling on him for a difficult explanation but excused herself. After all, this was early in the term and she would know more about each student's abilities later on.

Joan was something else. With a relatively high IQ, this student could be expected to cope with difficult, even abstract questions. Joan merely needed a bit of assistance in organizing her thoughts.

The following week, the teacher discovered that she had copied the IQ numbers incorrectly. She had aligned the roll book and the test score sheets, but one had probably shifted. The number after each student's name belonged to the next child.

While this tale is quite probably apocryphal, it has been retold in some version many times. The element of truth the story contains is the mysterious, almost unshakable, influence of IQ.

IQ and Intelligence

At the beginning of the century, in France, Alfred Binet and Theodore Simon created a written screening device for determining which children should continue with formal studies after high school. A decade or so later, in the United States, Lewis Terman of Stanford University reorganized that test and the result became known as the Stanford-Binet Intelligence Test, the standard for IQ testing.

David Wechsler, of New York City's Bellevue Hospital, between 1932 and 1967, authored his own test, the Wechsler-Bellevue Intelligence Scale. Its versions for children and adults have become widely used internationally. Many other tests have been devised and are also in extensive use throughout the world. These tests have undergone considerable polishing and, presumably, their accuracy has improved through the years. Intelligence tests are to psychologists what X rays are to physicians.

Despite their widespread use, not even the staunchest advocates claim perfection for any test. Most researchers treat intelligence quotients as imprecise measures but still an important indicator of intellectual capacity. Detractors not only denigrate these tests, but advocate their discontinuance.

Although IQ tests attempt to provide a quantified measure of cognitive depth, many psychologists acknowledge that they do not measure all of the important characteristics of intelligence. They fail, also, to weigh each measured characteristic fairly when determining an average. Since important aspects of intelligence are excluded, the skills measured may produce a distorted picture of a child's overall capability. No less an authority than the late Jean Piaget contended that all IQ tests did not measure all appropriate qualities. Earlier, J.P. Guilford, the celebrated psychologist, jolted the professional world by noting, with compelling logic, some 120 abilities related to each other in various degrees. Only a fraction of these are measured by IQ tests.

IQ Potency

Whatever its validity, the IQ shapes opinion. The intelligence quotient has become an integral factor in everyday as well as in professional judgments. If an IQ is known, it influences everybody: those who support it, those who have serious reservations about it, and those who would abolish it.

If an IQ is high, say 135, a teacher is apt to interpret the student's verbal responses and behavior in light of that score. The opposite case of underestimating a child's capabilities based on an IQ score is equally true and most unfortunate. Expectations of performance derived from IQ tests influence the child directly by the teacher's encouraging or ignoring the child.

Professionally, the IQ is merely a convenient method of determining an individual's standing within a group. Many educators prefer percentiles, the individual's score in relationship to the others through a given measuring instrument. Whatever the device, and no matter how the information is presented, a measure of a person's aptitude or knowledge, compared with other members of a group, affects opinions, even those of very knowledgeable people.

While presenting the case, how IQ influences opinion, to a graduate class in psychology, several students questioned me on both the efficacy of the score and its import. To establish my contention of "influence," I offered the group a hypothetical situation to consider.

Each student in this make-believe situation was to head a team of workers in an important project. The project, by its nature, required high levels of abstract thinking and general intellectual prowess. The students would be given a list of 100 applicants from which they were to select 10 for the effort. Along with other information on each applicant, an intelligence test result could be supplied upon request. Would the students wish to consider the scores to help them select their personnel?

All of the class members conceded that they would review the IQs, though some spoke of "putting them into a proper perspective." *The IQ indeed influences.*

Parents are not impervious to the power of the IQ. I have yet to hear a parent contend that the IQ of her child is too high, that the particular test is inaccurate, that her child is less intelligent than the score indicates and that the result should be brushed aside. IQ tests belong to a class of items that, once presented, cannot be ignored. For instance, in a court case, a witness for the prosecution blurts out, without being asked, that the accused had been arrested for crimes similar to the one now being charged. "He always beats the rap," adds the witness. The astonished defense attorney shouts "Objection!" repeatedly and the judge gavels a noisy courtroom back to order. "The jury," admonishes the judge, "will disregard that testimony. It is inadmissible!"

No way. The mind works differently. Although we can conjure up prescribed images at will, we can't easily suppress thoughts that have already arisen. And these thoughts affect our decisions. The legal system is well aware of this and has declared mistrials, if the violation is flagrant enough. The defendant gets a fresh opportunity to present his case without the tainted information as a factor.

Sets of preconceived notions exist in most people's minds that color and frequently cloud their thinking. Objectivity may be lost when a person is confronted with another's ethnicity, nationality, social status or education, religion, or age. Standby impressions, those based on earlier assumptions or experiences, are summoned to the fore to be matched with accents or speech patterns.

In the courtroom example, most jurors, try as they might, could not set aside completely the thought that the defendant had been accused of similar crimes in the past. Anyone might be unlucky enough to appear guilty because of an unfortunate confluence of circumstances but, the reasonable juror asks, how many times?

The IQ is a perfect example of an influencing agent. Psychologists, educators, and laypeople have all incorporated this score into their evaluative processes. The accuracy of the IQ may be questionable but, once known, cannot be dismissed. A teacher cannot ignore a child's IQ any more than a juror can disregard "inadmissible evidence."

The debate over intelligence test scores continues and many volumes have been produced relating to the subject, but the topic here is the underachiever. To know whether your child is truly an underachiever, you have to know his potential. He is achieving if he is performing at or above his genetic expectations. He is underachieving if he performs below his ability and is not handicapped by some physical, emotional, or environmental condition. A factor in the equation is his true capability, which is exactly what the IQ test attempts to reveal. The IQ or any substitute test is your child's ability "by the numbers."

The IQ and Your Child

Library shelves almost bow from the weight of books expressing the myriad views and reviews about intelligence testing. Interest in the measurement of intellect extends beyond professionals and captures a large audience when presented on television, in books or articles. An IQ score, *in conjunction with other evidence,* will help you determine if your child is an underachiever or not and is therefore an important tool. As a busy parent, you may simply read the following, which will place the IQ in its proper perspective. Please consider each item only as it relates to your child.

- IQ tests used by the schools are *developed meticulously* and tested on thousands of children before being marketed.
- Researchers argue over whether the IQ score measures the *inherent mental capacity* of the child or the results of his *learning*. Neither proposition changes the outcome of the educator's experience. The score has proven to be a worthwhile *estimate of* the child's *academic potential*.
- The notion that IQ tests measure the skills needed in school is supported by the performance of the students. Since Binet based his original work on exercises used by French teachers, this is hardly surprising. The tests lose much of their predictive power for success rates beyond school. These results confirm the notion that tests measure the characteristics needed for academics, but disregard other important areas of the intellect.
- No one has equal abilities in all areas. If charted, individual strengths take the shape of a mountain range—peaks and valleys. The IQ is designed to provide an average which can be misleading. A child might be outstanding in dealing with mathematical abstractions but not able to write with clarity. Averaging the two capabilities would reveal little about each.
- Powerful arguments exist that IQs err by omission. Tests do not measure every known attribute of intelligence and do not claim to do so. Your child may have some very usable strengths not measured by the standard test.
- One factor, standing alone, cannot be equated with a person's intelligence. Consider the retarded savants who perform a given feat with unbelievable proficiency. These are extreme examples, but children with a propensity to perform at one or two areas significantly above the average of their other abilities are not so rare.
- Intelligence in humans is an involved mixture of individual and overlapping intellectual abilities. Psychologists have not agreed on a definition of intelli-

gence. Professors used to teach, without intending humor, that intelligence is what the intelligence test measures. Even if there were a consensus, no one would know whether the various characteristics were fixed or moldable, genetic or learned.

- Many intelligence test detractors claim a cultural bias is built into the tests. Altered tests, designed to make them culture free/fair have not, as yet, satisfied these critics. The cultural bias controversy has no relevancy in determining if your child is an underachiever as that term is defined herein.
- IQ tests and similar standardized examinations do not measure motivation or the general attitude of the child. The child's approach to school is a major factor in his success.
- Parents can be confident that a child with a high IQ can master any reasonable school subject. Children do not score high on these tests by chance. An elevated level indicates that the child is competent in abilities necessary for academics.

Wrap-Up

Knowledge about a child's IQ affects attitudes, school placement, and a child's self-view. The IQ influences virtually everyone's view on the intelligence of a child and only rarely can be dismissed.

Intelligence tests in general use are highly sophisticated measuring instruments and offer good indications of a child's potential for academic performance. IQs provide one important bit of evidence for parents trying to assess their child's capabilities. Since the tests do not measure all of a child's intellectual abilities, the parent should take other attributes into account. *Look beyond the numbers.*

3

Beyond the Numbers

Two Wrongs Making a Right

"What do you think, Bill? Will she be able to do the job?"

Bill Lisbone, the assistant superintendent in charge of professional personnel, pondered his boss's question. If he favored the appointment of Liz Mintway as the elementary supervisor and she didn't work out, the superintendent would hold him accountable. "You must be responsible for the decisions you make," his boss had declared many times. You weren't supposed to hedge with the school superintendent. You investigated, you thought, and then made a definite commitment. You were then on record for the position you'd taken.

"I think, sir, that the odds are in her favor. I observed her three times in the classroom and she related extremely well to her kids. Every principal has given her a top rating. The recommendations from the other administrators are not ambivalent. She's good. My vote is for her. I don't see how we can go wrong."

The superintendent then turned to the retiring elementary school supervisor. "Well, Barbara. Can Mintway take your place?"

"No one can take my place," quipped the older woman.

"Okay, Barbara. I know. You're one of a kind. But do you . . ."

"We're all one of a kind," she interrupted.

The school official held his hands up in mock surrender. "Barbara, we are going to miss you. But, really. You've looked at Mintway's records, you've read the recommendations, you've observed her in the classroom and you've been in at the interviews. Can she do the job as well as, that is, almost as well as you did?"

"No."

"No?"

"What do you want, an answer that'll last forever? I've had twenty-three years of experience supervising. Give her ten years or so and she'll be in my category. Maybe. But if you're asking if she can do a creditable job for a beginner, the answer is yes."

Liz Mintway was appointed to the position of elementary school supervisor for her district.

In addition to a title, she was given a generous salary increase, an office in the administrative building and the part-time services of a secretary. Her promotion was based on teaching experience, an earned master's degree, recommendations, and two interviews with the school superintendent and some of his staff. No one knew or even thought of asking her IQ. The determination was made on criteria which were unrelated to intelligence test results, the numbers.

The teacher, now a supervisor, did very well relating to six-, seven-, and eight-year-olds. She had some trouble adjusting to older children, especially to sixth-graders, but she was expected to overcome this difficulty in time. Ms. Mintway exhibited her talent doing demonstration lessons for teachers, particularly the new ones. The fact that she was a talented instructor was never questioned. Everything else she did was.

The supervising role required the new appointee to address groups of professional staff and parents, lead a curriculum development conference, and edit a school district paper. Her training and experience were limited to a narrow band of pursuits and her ability to adapt to these new duties proved inadequate.

All employers make similar errors in hiring and promoting. The district could have given this teacher an intelligence test but that would have revealed nothing helpful. Liz Mintway had a superior IQ. What she didn't have was superior talent in all vital supervisory areas. By misreading her capabilities, the district failed to fill a vital position and lost a fine teacher. Ms. Mintway resigned.

Bill Lisbone was ready when told his boss wanted to see him. He knew what to expect. The chief officer of the district handed him the elementary supervisor's written notice and just waited—in silence.

The assistant screened his words carefully. "As you know, she wasn't doing very well, anyhow. I made a mistake in nominating her but, on the plus side, she left of her own accord. Now we can fill the position with someone else."

"How wonderful," sneered the superintendent. "What great applicants do you have to offer now?"

"Actually none, at the moment." The assistant's preparation for this meeting was now paying dividends. He had called various district administrators, asked for, and received recommendations and records.

"I have a Mrs. Anna Schmidt, a veteran teacher with a fine reputation."

He handed his superior a folder containing the teacher's official history. "She seems to have everything we need but doesn't meet the academic requirements for the job, which is good."

The superintendent looked at him quizzically. He then held his right hand out, palm up, as if to say "Explain."

"I suggest that she be given the position on a temporary basis. That will give us all the time needed to find someone else even if it means searching outside the district. When we do find the right person, Mrs. Schmidt, who lacks a certificate, can be returned to the classroom. We'll make everything very clear at the beginning."

The story didn't end as planned. The superintendent agreed with his assistant's scheme and Mrs. Schmidt gladly accepted the assignment. At this writing, 11 years have passed. She now has all of the paper qualifications and hardly anyone remembers using the label "temporary." The superintendent is gone and his replacement, D. William Lisbone, claims Anna Schmidt is the finest elementary school supervisor in the state.

Parental Judgment

The IQ provides an estimate of a child's academic potential but, as a parent, you should look for more. *You might find areas of strength in your child that the school will not uncover.* You might also find some characteristic that your child should not rely on. All of the tests, track records, and observations, even in the hands of experts, may not produce the predicted results. Ms. Mintway, in another district, is still a fine teacher. That in itself does not make her a good supervisor of teachers. Mrs. Schmidt, who had never prepared herself for a supervisory position, once the opportunity arose, displayed her competence.

Parents have a necessary but difficult challenge. *Identify strengths and lack of strengths in your child.* Your child should develop all of his innate abilities while learning to avoid the unnecessary misfortune of a Mintway. Look at all the evidence obtainable, but, at some point, you must make a judgment call.

The Enigma of Intelligence

Defining intelligence in a manner that encompasses all of its uses is as difficult as determining a precise definition for pornography. The Supreme Court, itself, has hedged on defining obscene items by referring to some vague concept known as community standards. Politicians, following the court's lead, have learned to equivocate by adopting one critic's observation on prurient material. "I can't put it into words, but I know it when I see it." The same befuddled observation is applicable to mental capacity. Intelligence defies precise definitions, but you recognize it when you see it.

The layperson has less difficulty defining intelligence than the professional. The psychologist can dissect any definition and note, with impressive logic, areas of mental activity where the definition falls short. To cover most possibilities, a definition would have to follow the lead lawyers find necessary and fill pages with the equivalent of "Whereas . . ." Such a definition would be too unwieldy for practical purposes and, no matter how involved, still subject to valid criticism.

Yet, in this work, we still require a working definition to complete our equation for determining underachievement. Therefore, for our purpose, we define intelligence as the efficient application of skill, knowledge, and experience to new situations. This includes organizing seemingly disparate objects and events into a pattern for understanding and solving problems. Or, as a 12-year-old underachiever once expressed it, "Use what you've learned to get by."

Intelligence: Determination by Perception

While a consensus on a definition for intelligence evades the professional's grasp, it is, nevertheless, understood on a daily basis by everyone. You already have impressions of people you know—family, friends, neighbors, and co-workers. In your everyday life, you meet new people all the time. You talk to people in stores, on the street, in church, at restaurants, on trains, and in a hundred other places. You form impressions.

Perceptions, however, can delude because the characteristics of intelligence are deceiving. While observational techniques differ and considerations vary, there is some commonality. As a general rule, people are influenced by memory, word facility, voice, and mannerisms. A person's occupation is also a factor. Without conscious effort, we tend to rate people by their position: physician, judge, cab driver, salesperson, professor, journalist, waitress.

Withholding judgment may be difficult. Could the middle-aged dishwasher in the cafeteria be an astronomer picking up some extra cash? How many people of average intellect have passed the bar exam, entered West Point, or scored high enough on the Miller's Analogy or like test to warrant admission to a doctoral program? It does happen, perhaps, but not too often.

Inaccurate Instant Evaluation

Reserving judgment on a person's ability in important matters can help avoid unpleasant situations. In going beyond the numbers, one must not estimate a person's ability based on one observed talent.

The guest speaker for an audience is not necessarily the most intelligent. The wittiest, the most poised, composed, or prepared person at a meeting is not necessarily the most intelligent. Characteristics such as these may be deceptive.

People speak well because of an inherent capacity or practice. They may not be intimidated by interviewers, cameras, unusual situations, or audiences. Some people are natural "hams" who enjoy the spotlight. They are then at their best in these circumstances. However, these images are *not* hard evidence of how they will perform behind the administrator's desk or in the research laboratory. A good public speaker should be recognized as a good public speaker. She may not be a good physician, engineer, or psychologist. The quick-witted man in a debate may deflate his opponent with a sharp barb or timely pun and gain a laugh or applause from the audience, but that doesn't necessarily make him a sage, or even right.

Interestingly, there are people with commanding personalities who present worthwhile arguments, stimulate and hold audiences, and convince listeners of their logic, but cannot write. Generally, there are two types of people who have difficulty communicating by the written word. First is the group who fail at writing, especially in school, because of an unpleasant childhood experience. The second group only *seems* to do well when speaking. When their speeches are transcribed and examined, many inconsistencies, dubious approaches, spurious arguments, and unfulfilled early promises become apparent.

A person who speaks well may be as competent as he sounds, but it "ain't necessarily so." People who impress orally may or may not be as intelligent as perceived. If they are not, employers, by accepting them on this basis alone, are apt to sustain a loss. Even if a person speaks and writes well, he still may lack leadership qualities, such as perseverance and broad understanding.

Intelligence comes in many forms. A danger arises in selecting people to perform in a given situation on the basis of incorrect or limited criteria. As a parent, you should evaluate your own youngster with as wide a range of criteria as you can gather.

You should not rely on test scores (the numbers) alone, but go beyond them. Children tend to display special aptitudes early in life. Those who exhibit inclinations toward reading, music, dance, art, athletics, mechanical assembly, and any other desirable trait, should be encouraged to develop them. Your child, before and during his school years, should recognize and utilize his strengths to achieve success. Some weaknesses can be improved, but humans will always be deficient in some areas. The child should learn about his own attributes and learn to employ them strategically.

A Mrs. Mintway, even as an intelligent adult, failed to understand her limitations. She could have sought and attained a promotion in a position requiring the strengths she possessed. Mrs. Schmidt, on the other hand, wasn't even trying to utilize her gifts and became a supervisor only through circumstances that, for her, were fortunate.

Wrap-Up

Fall back on your own resources to determine your child's ability. In so doing, go beyond the intelligence quotient. Remember:

1. The definition of intelligence is debatable. There are many abilities, some ill understood.
2. Ability in a given area does not guarantee equal abilities in other, even related, areas.
3. Everyone, including the experts, has difficulty predicting a person's performance. Experienced administrators do a creditable job, but not always. Mistakes are made.
4. As a parent, you may be somewhat biased in your evaluation of your child but you need not be blind to

reality. No one can do everything. There will be some things your child can't do. You do not want to doom your child to failure.
5. Identify the strong characteristics in your child that may be developed into rewarding strengths.
6. Seek the highest level of achievement and satisfaction your child can attain comfortably.

4

Grading May Not Reflect True Performance

A Problem So Common

Adele can present a litany of problems without apparent solutions. She is the single parent of two elementary school-children. Her job is her only source of income. Her husband, after years of alcoholism, wandered off to places unknown. He has been gone now for three years—no support and no communication. She doesn't know if he is alive and tells herself she doesn't care.

Her son, Wally, is 11 and in sixth grade, and her daughter, Meg, is eight years old and in third grade. Adele rises early to prepare her children for school. She leaves the house before them and returns about an hour after they do. A neighbor, for pay, comes to her house during these hours of absence. Though Adele is able to bear the cost of this adult supervision, she cannot afford the additional expense of domestic services. The household chores are hers to do, alone.

Wally's mother has adjusted to being a busy parent. She has developed efficient systems for meeting her obligations. She avoids complaining, which she points out, only bores people, except for one gnawing and vexing subject. She discusses that with colleagues and friends. Adele is concerned about Wally's grades in school. She knows by the numbers and the signs she observes that he is a bright child, but his report card is saturated with C's. Adele feels guilt about having an underachieving child and frustrated at having no solutions. She is a certified elementary schoolteacher.

The evidence available to this parent does not support the underachieving label for Wally. He does not dislike school any more than his friends who do considerably better. He does not seek to avoid school. He does not excuse himself from doing homework, studying for tests, and engaging in extra school work. He seems to be applying himself, willingly. He is a poor performer, though he shouldn't be.

Perplexed, the boy's mother presents the case to the school psychologist whom she knows slightly. After listening to the child's history, the psychologist concludes that Wally has been unable to adjust to his father's drinking and subsequent disappearance.

"However, Adele, although all the evidence seems to fit this explanation, we'd better be sure. Why don't you arrange to have him see a clinical psychologist who is more familiar with emotional problems. I'll provide a school history and whatever else is needed."

After Wally has consulted with the psychologist several times, Adele knows immediately that the news about her son is not bad. She has learned years before that the facial expression and greeting of a professional to the family of the "patient" provides the bottom line. Now, at the university's psychological clinic, Wally's examiner waits for her with a smile followed by a firm handshake. No limp fingers. No solemnity. The results, she feels certain, are positive.

The psychologist, after careful testing, concludes that the original diagnosis was incorrect. Wally thinks about his father and worries about his mother, but no serious disturbance is involved. The young man is well adjusted to his life. He accepts his lack of good grades as something that is unavoidable. The boy's explanation?

"I guess I'm not as smart as my mother thinks I am."

The psychologist contends that Wally is just an under-achiever; one of those kids who, because of interest concentrated elsewhere, or a growing stage, or a personality flaw, doesn't do well in a formal setting. The explanation doesn't satisfy Adele. No one is "just" an underachiever. Nothing else in his personality or actions corroborates the flaw, or the stage, or the intense outside interest.

This frustrated parent knows there could be other reasons, such as teacher partiality, peer competition, or misplacement. None of these seems right either. The explanation comes later, from a nonprofessional source.

An Answer

To Adele, her son is an enigma. To the school system, he is a statistic. His mother finds this very discomforting.

Once a riddle is explained, the answer becomes obvious. "I should have known or at least suspected that," Adele stated. "The big clue was there all the time. Wally's friends, all good students, considered my son their equal. Their attitude showed in the conversations I overheard and in their common ventures. They kept coming to our house to do homework. In fact, unless I'm being deluded by parental bias, they seemed to look up to Wally, at least a bit.

"If I were missing something, and of course I was, I thought that maybe they could provide a lead."

One late Saturday morning, the anxious mother addressed the two young boys waiting for Wally to change his clothes. "Jeff. Kevin. You know Wally. You're both good friends. Why do you think he doesn't do well in school?"

The boys appeared surprised that Wally's mother, a teacher, should ask them. Both shrugged. They had nothing to offer. Adele pursued the inquiry with a series of questions starting with, "Is it . . . ?" She then enumerated, one by one, all of the general possibilities, though she was already sure of the responses. The boys showed their discomfiture as they supplied the negatives. Adele dropped the subject. No help here.

As the adult rose and started toward the kitchen, Jeff mentioned, as if everyone knew and it hadn't been worth explaining, "Wally's no good at tests." In one casual observation a child cleared the clouds. The teacher in Adele knew immediately. The thesis didn't have to be confirmed. It was so obvious, it had to be correct. And it was.

More Than Realized

Wally is actually doing better than the evaluative criteria used in grading indicate, but one important skill is severely blemished. Wally has trouble doing well on written tests, a performance defect not too uncommon. He arrives prepared at test day and, based on his knowledge of the material to be tested, he should do well. The testing milieu, however, has become what I call an affective dissonant. At test time, Wally's emotions become unbridled and hamper his thinking. He is unable to organize and utilize his cognitive resources in an effective manner. His mental motor fails to fire all its cylinders.

Is Wally an underachiever? He is. He is an underachiever because one vital element needed for achievement is impaired. One rung in his ladder of learning is broken. Comprehensive learning includes the capability of using the skills and knowledge mastered when required.

The Teachers' Side of Marking

Donna, a first-year teacher, realizes, too late, the coffee is very hot, but swallows it rather than suffer the embarrassment of spitting it out. She says nothing for the moment but pretends to listen as her elementary supervisor and another colleague, Valerie, exchange views on yesterday's parent-teacher meeting. As the irritation in her mouth and throat subsides, the novice dabs her eyes with a tissue.

"Anything wrong, Donna?" asks her obviously concerned co-worker.

"No. I just have something in my eye. It's okay now. I'm sorry. What were you saying?"

"I had this interesting talk with Mrs. Valkin about her daughter, Mary Ann. She couldn't understand why *her little girl* couldn't get straight A's."

"What did you tell her?" questions the supervisor.

"Well, I said 'I gave her what she earned. She really did quite well. Is there a problem?'"

"Sure there's a problem. You gave *her little girl,* a straight-A student, some B's," the supervisor adds, with just enough sarcasm to show this was an old story.

The rookie of the group, with the burning in her mouth now reduced to a tingle, wonders why they were even having this discussion. It doesn't seem too important to her. She says so.

"Donna, whether little Mary, or whatever her name is, earns all A's, or just A's and B's, may not affect the rain forests or clear the polluted lakes, but to her mother, *it is important,*" explains the supervisor. She is suddenly serious. No hint of sarcasm is detectable.

"Oh, I didn't mean to disparage . . ."

"Hold it. We don't do everything right and we get blamed for every wrong, but there's not a teacher in this school who doesn't weigh every mark very carefully. I know.

"I'm not going to preach about responsibility and all that, but look at it this way. We have the most precious commodities there are. Children. You and I won't lose any sleep over Mary Ann's grades, but think what they mean to the child and her mother. Every mark is important. There is a difference between a B and an A and the kid wants an A."

Turning to the veteran teacher, the supervisor says, "So go on, Valerie, what happened next?"

"Mrs. Valkin suggested that maybe some marks were a mere guess. I said 'No. Not a guess, a judgment.' Then I pulled out all the tests and showed her how I had arrived at each grade."

It sounds like H & R Block talking to the IRS, Donna thinks. She remains quiet.

"You're known for your patience," comments the supervisor.

"You have to be patient. You have to explain things right the first time," the supervisor explains to Donna.

"And," the supervisor adds, "you have to have good supporting evidence for the marks you give. Otherwise an angry parent can give you fits."

Before Donna can respond with a question, Valerie

starts to talk. "Speaking of grades, my Justin came home with two C's on his report card."

Donna waits but the others say nothing. She feels compelled to break the silence. "What did you do?"

"Why, I put on my best irate-parent manner and went to see that teacher!"

Justin's mother finishes her coffee and leaves Donna and the supervisor alone to confer.

"Grades, you know, are extremely important. They determine school decisions for placement and tell the parent how well the child is doing. You have to use your judgment in grading but you need some hard evidence, too," says the supervisor.

"Tests," said Donna.

"Right. Let's talk for a minute about tests. Subjective tests, you know, the essay type, are so easy to make and so time-consuming to evaluate. I guess you had a course in testing. Read all the tests first to get an overall impression. Then go back and read each one again to grade it. It sounds good but takes forever."

"I think I like objective tests," Donna notes.

"Sure. Easy to grade. True-False. Multiple-choice. Fill in the blanks. Complete the sentence, and so on. But wait until you have to make up such tests. Each question has to be clear and represent some part of the study unit. A monumental task."

"What do you suggest?"

"Some of each. Tests are a must. Expect to spend a lot of time on them. That's a part of our job the public doesn't see."

Teachers do spend considerable time creating and marking tests. Teacher-made examinations provide the teacher with valuable information about the progress of the class as a whole and individual students. The competent teacher uses a test as a traffic light. If the class has done well, the light is green and she continues on to the next lesson. Poor results, of course, are the red light. The teacher now plans review and reinforcement material for the class. The test also spotlights individual children who need special help.

Parents have the right to question grades and teachers should willingly produce the tests that helped her make the grading decisions. In a later chapter, tests will be shown to be a useful tool to help parents help their children to learn.

The Wallys Considered

Wally's mother pondered her child's problem. Certainly his poor grades were the result of low test scores, but perhaps his substandard performance was not due to lack of learning. Maybe he just couldn't, as his friend Jeff suggested, do well on tests.

Although Wally is an extreme case, poor test performance measured against actual learning is rather common. A child who loses just 10% by ineffectual test-taking abilities is likely to be an underachiever.

Tests may affect the student in many ways. A child may:

- "Freeze" when confronted with a test. He sees the paper; he holds a writing instrument; his muscles await orders; his mind is stuck in neutral.
- Associate tests with some unpleasant experience. One youngster was caught copying from a neighbor during a test and was sternly reprimanded in front of the class. The image of that traumatic episode returned whenever he stared at a test paper. He had difficulty concentrating.
- Fear writing an answer the teacher could criticize. He may lack self-esteem and be unable to attack the problem vigorously. Many such children search for a "safe" answer instead of responding with a more creative choice.
- Focus on one part of the examination. Not knowing how to budget his time could cause him to turn in unfinished papers.
- Express himself poorly under pressure. He may block out the words and phrases he needs. His vocabulary returns after the test, like an old friend who was absent when needed.

Other Considerations on Grading

The equation for the determination of underachievement depends in part on a child's in-class performance. The evaluation of his work is the responsibility of the teacher who must and should rely heavily on tests.

Grades are generally fair and usually reasonably accurate. As a parent, you should not assume, however, that they are flawless. If all the pieces don't mesh, if you have some suspicions about your child's marks, you should investigate.

Some considerations related to report card grades are:

- No one has offered a totally equitable and accurate system to grade students that accounts for all of the vagaries possible.
- Attempts to replace the typical marking system with a simple pass-fail report have merit in some situations, but haven't satisfied the students, parents, or teachers.
- Replacing letter grades with check marks or other symbols doesn't help. Teachers start adding a plus to a check and, before long, the replaced system is back, with different configurations.
- Written comments, especially in the elementary grades, are desirable but become burdensome. Teachers can, and do, buy books with comments already prepared. Canned comments, presumably, will soon be computerized.
- Teachers are influenced by the general caliber of the students in the class or in the school, which may be higher or lower than the norm. Transfer a B student from an advanced class to one for average children and, without extra effort, said child will probably earn A's.
- Teachers tend to instruct at the level of their class and mark accordingly. College admission officers are familiar with the high schools in their state; they base their evaluations of grade averages on the student's school.
- Teachers have pets or children they like better than others. Most teachers try not to let this affect their thinking, but, of course, teachers are homo sapiens, too.

- A teacher's expectations of a child may influence the child's class performance. A child's appearance, demeanor, IQ, background, or record could affect the evaluation. For instance, one teacher, informed that a child had been caught cheating on two earlier occasions, always looked at the student with suspicion. She did not, she stated, allow her grading to be swayed by this fact. Perhaps.

Wrap-Up

Grades are usually a reliable measurement of your child's appearance, but certainly not in every case. If the pieces don't fit, take a closer look.

Teachers care. Act accordingly.

Progress is measured by judging performance and by tests. The teacher uses both. You should too.

Using a number or symbol for a letter changes little. Whatever is used should provide information about your child's progress in each area and suggestions for helping him to improve.

Many children are not adept at test-taking. Their emotional involvement or lack of technique imposes a severe penalty. The results are reflected in their grades.

A grade or a grade average substantially below a child's ability level is a danger signal. A corrective program is indicated.

PART II

CAUSES:
IDENTIFY YOUR CHILD

5

The Fear of Failing

The Failure Syndrome

A negative attitude toward schoolwork encompasses more than a sense of frustration. The child learns that failure can be humiliating. The possibility of not doing well becomes a fear in itself—a fear of failure.

The syndrome is not limited to children. Adults may also be plagued by the same perturbance, usually a continuation of childhood patterns. The young and mature alike display a reluctance to engage in activities without reasonable guarantees of obscurity should they fail.

The fear of failure, in many circumstances, is devastating. When confronted with questionable outcomes, the child or adult harboring these feelings avoids participating. He can't take chances. He can't commit. He wants the world to think he doesn't try because he isn't interested.

As a student, the fear-laden child may not study. His reasoning: If he prepared and failed, he would demonstrate an inability to do the work. If he doesn't study, he establishes a valid reason for failing.

The young child may doubt he is as smart as his parents believe. Not succeeding could cost him the respect (love) of his parents. He may avoid efforts that could expose him to failure.

A child may strive for success in subjects where he feels more confident. He may even overachieve in these areas as he attempts to compensate for the tasks he shirks.

The underachieving child may feign laziness to mask his feelings of uncertainty. He may find reasons why he can't do the work, or even try. When forced to make an effort, he gives up easily, allows almost anything to distract his attention, and blames others for not completing his work. He usually demands that success be instantaneous. He hides his fear of failure by rejecting school.

The adult with fear of failure is imbued with, but camouflages, the same propensities. When an option exists, he may elect to avoid exposing himself to ''disgrace-by-failure.''

This misgiving was exemplified by a well-qualified teacher who had prepared herself for a principal's examination in a large urban school district. She was bright, knowledgeable, experience, and possessed all of the necessary degrees and certificates. She also enjoyed the praise of her peers and her administrators. Somewhere, concealed in her subconscious, lived the memory of an earlier, devastating defeat. She recoiled from exposing herself to a similar encounter. A well-adjusted person would have asked, ''What do I have to lose?'' This woman had ''face'' to lose. She rationalized that she really didn't want to be a principal. She was really content in her present position. She had no need of a promotion. Her ego required no such nourishment. Thus, she never took the test. By avoiding the possibility of a failure her colleagues would know about, she curtailed her own ambitions and capped her career.

The fear of failing inhibits many people at all levels and pursuits who might have risen to more rewarding positions. Adults, on occasion, unshackle themselves from this yoke, but not typically. The time to overcome these deeply ingrained misgivings is during childhood.

Despite a high level of native intelligence, many youngsters, experiencing frequent academic frustration, assume a posture of hopelessness. The signs of such a discouraging outlook are familiar to parents of underachieving children. Do any of the following statements describe your child?

- He offers both routine and imaginative reasons for postponing an assignment.

- Having exhausted his excuses for procrastinating, he hesitates more than a justifiable period before actually beginning his work.
- Once started, he discovers that essential materials, such as pencils or books, are not at his study place. He retrieves these slowly—one at a time.
- After an initial effort, he looks around as if hoping for a last-minute reprieve.
- When finally immersed in his work, he examines each item of the assignment with hesitation, as if probing for unclean or poisoned food.
- He displays gestures of helplessness, expressions of puzzlement, and comments of despair. The work is beyond him.
- He is indifferent to his progress but aware of the clock.
- He drifts off to a reverie and must be reminded to return to work.
- He surrenders to the first obstacle.

Failure can become a habit, a pattern of behavior that quickly becomes a routine. A child who continues to fail may just give up. He ceases to make an honest effort to master his assignments.

Other causes may be responsible for the same behavior as the fear of failing. However, this inner uncertainty is far more widespread than generally acknowledged. Not many people admit they avoid activities that could expose their weakness. "No, I'm not going to take the principal's examination because if I don't pass everyone will look down on me."

You will hear the same explanation but disguised as something else. "No, I'm not taking the test because I wouldn't want the job if it were offered."

From children you get:

"I'm not interested."
"I don't care."
"It's baby stuff."
"I could do it if I wanted to. I just don't want to."

Causes Unlimited

Many possible explanations exist for children trying to shy away from the possibility of stumbling or becoming indifferent to academic learning. Most of these reasons stem from some type of very negative experience in the background of the child. The parents, in these cases, were either uninvolved, or their initiatives had a negative effect. The next chapter provides a sampling of incidents which have affected children. Similar ones may have had impact on your child. Your awareness of these possibilities could be helpful. A list might include:

- Disappointment
- Embarrassment
- Disillusionment
- Victimization
- Ridicule
- Rivalry
- Partiality
- Physiological differences
- Social failures

Parental misdirection is sometimes a factor. The parent attempts to help the child but, unintentionally, causes harm. Three examples, all debatable in professional quarters, follow.

Pushing or Elevating?

A heated dispute gaining in controversy is over early academic training for preschool and kindergarten children. One side advocates the introduction of school subjects at the earliest possible time. As you might expect, many commercial enterprises supplying books, audiovisual materials and programs, as well as schools for early childhood, support this view. They do not stand alone, however. A large number of respected professionals hold the same position. The benefits they see include:

- A chance for the child to recognize his own potential and develop confidence in his abilities

- An early enrichment opportunity in the age of complex technology, high-speed travel, and instant global communication
- A system to offset the disadvantages of economically deprived children

The detractors are growing in number or at least becoming more vocal. They note the dangers based on *some* children *not* being *physically* or *emotionally ready* to cope with academic tasks. They speak of inadequately developed eye movement and/or fine-motor coordination and attention spans too short for the work required. Boys, they point out, may lag behind girls by six months in the developmental process. The resulting deficits may include:

- A tendency toward emotional disturbance
- Continuing attention problems
- Later learning problems
- Aggressiveness
- Self-doubt
- Stifled enthusiasm
- Tension
- Childhood burnout

When Jean Piaget, the century's master of child maturation, was asked if his theories could be used to accelerate the cognitive and affective growth of children, he responded, "Why would you want to?"

The premature forcing of a child into a formal educational format, say these critics, may be more detrimental than beneficial. The early start may not provide the advantageous edge sought by parents. Problems can be avoided if children are placed at an appropriate level at the right time.

Michael, age five, was enrolled in a kindergarten that stressed academic learning. Most of the children in the group responded well in this learning situation, but Michael was not yet ready for the pressure of discipline or inflexible routines. The child could not sit still. His limited ability to concentrate interfered with his learning. The youngster became a behavioral problem. Michael was not unusual. A child forced to attend beyond the comfortable limits of his ability may react in some disquieting fashion.

The consequences of mandated academic learning for a child not quite ready may result in later learning problems. Children forced into situations which require self-reliance may not perform well. They may not yet have developed coping mechanisms that support responsibility. Forcing the situation can result in the child's becoming an underachiever.

If your youngster in grade school exhibits the characteristics described above, you should review his early exposure to regulated education. If he has, indeed, been exposed to programs beyond his readiness level, his enrollment has been counterproductive. Fortunately, he will likely respond to the same remedial measures as other underachieving children.

If you have another child who is at an appropriate age for early study, you have a decision to make. *Your child* may be one of these youngsters who could profit from such a curriculum. Perhaps the following considerations of what you should do may help you decide:

1. Recognize that both sides of the early childhood disagreement lack compelling evidence, based on tightly designed longitudinal studies, to support their views.
2. Evaluate your *child as an individual.* Your own childhood experience and that of others may not be relevant.
3. *Ask questions* about the learning facility for your child. Accept no vague answers. Determine who *administers* and who *instructs* what *program.* Do the personnel have the training and experience to implement a well-defined curriculum?
4. *Watch your child,* if enrolled, for progress or signs of tension. If he is happy, eager, and learning, let him fly. If he shows signs of unusual irritability, sleeplessness, or misbehavior, you may have to withdraw him.
5. Remember that:
   a. Children can usually assimilate more than expected but playtime should not be curtailed. Play is a child's work and an essential form of learning.
   b. A balance of activities is necessary for all children.

Don't push the child hard into a particular direction.
Don't stop him, either, if his choice is acceptable.

The reader may have become aware that I'm sitting on the
fence on this issue—not my usual position. I'm not sure formal,
academic-type preschool programs are helpful. They certainly
are not for all children.

Overindulging

Somewhat related to parental misdirection is the overin-
dulged child. The parent who wants to give the young child
everything may cause the youngster to become trouble-prone
later on. The pupil who assumes, lacking a basis of comparison, that he is entitled to everything he wants may be
confronted with a harsh reality once he enters school. His
teacher is not likely to indulge him the way his parents do. The
child becomes confused when he doesn't receive the unearned
recognition and rewards he is used to getting. If he wants to
distribute the milk but the teacher selects someone else, if he
raises his hand to answer a question but the teacher calls on
another child, his performance in school may be affected. Most
children, even ego-inflated ones, absorb such shocks without
much damage, but some develop a distaste for school. This
disaffection could develop into underachievement.

Using the Wrong Remediation

Diane's parents were dissatisfied with her schoolwork. They
were certain that the fourth-grader could do considerably
better. The nine-year-old's teacher thought so too. Rather than
a haphazard approach to get the child on course, the parents
decided to design and implement a plan.

They acted in unison. Diane was never made aware of any
disagreement. They scheduled and held family meetings,
explaining their observations, the views of the school, and
Diane's future. Poor school performance, they emphasized,
would limit the satisfaction she would gain from life.

After establishing why learning was important, they began

planning her education. Diane's study time was increased each evening and hours were set aside each Saturday for review of the work completed during the week. They helped with problems but also set firm rules. She was never to fall behind in any subject, never to attend school unprepared, and was to report everything that went on during the school day.

The plan was based on standard practices, but it didn't work. Diane's performance remained at a constant level. The parents tried encouragement and lectures but without success. They resorted to threats followed by punishment. Again, they had no success.

The young girl felt the punishment was unjustified and said so repeatedly. She resented being deprived of privileges available to her friends. When the school reported that Diane was misbehaving, her parents became alarmed. They cancelled the punishments. The girl's behavior returned to normal but her academic efforts did not. She now operated at a lower level than when they had initiated their plan.

Remedial programs, to be effective, must account for a child's overall needs and feelings. Gut feelings and ill-informed advice are insufficient. *Lectures and punishments may have a place but they're not the foundation of a good program.*

Wrap-Up

The fear of failure is far more commonplace than generally recognized. Children and adults, both, fabricate reasons for avoiding challenges rather than admitting to apprehension about not succeeding. This fear is usually based on earlier negative experiences.

Sometimes parents, through misdirection, inadvertently cause a distressing experience.

1. Formal early childhood education programs are advocated by many as the means to help the individual child leap to a quick and solid start. Others decry the belief, claiming such involvement could be injurious to the child. Both sides have some data to support their view. Neither group has enough, however, possibly because some children benefit while others are harmed. Parents must decide themselves about their own child and observe and gauge his progress.

2. Parents sometimes do overindulge their child by providing too much. The child does not learn to earn what he wants and his expectations of reward become too high. He then faces a different situation in school and may have difficulty in adjusting.

3. Parents sometimes err by assuming that their child merely needs more discipline and study time to overcome underperformance. In these cases, the cure may be worse than the ailment. Parents should, instead, follow a comprehensive remedial plan that focuses on the causes of underachievement and provides the methodology to bring about the desired changes.

6

Has Your Child Been Turned Off?

Disappointments

Children may develop a negative attitude toward school at any age for an unlimited number of reasons. Six-year-old Lee expressed disappointment in the first grade.

"You told me I would like first grade. I don't. Why did you tell me that?"

Youngsters have a penchant for remembering whatever their parents would like them to forget. Lee had tired of kindergarten and complained to his mother. He was showing more and more of a reluctance to go. The parent, wishing to avert a problem, explained that kindergarten was a step into regular school, where the big boys go. Lee would enjoy the first grade. The child accepted his mother's explanation but from time to time required reassurance.

"Will I really like first grade?"

"Yes, dear. You certainly will."

The matter seemed simple enough and resolved. Lee stopped complaining about kindergarten and, since the summer was placed between the grades, his mother felt he would enter school refreshed and eager after his vacation. She was right. He entered school in the fall, fresh, eager, and anticipating.

Lee realized quickly that his expectations would not be met. He didn't enjoy first grade. He tried arguing with his mother but dropped the issue after he realized there was no choice. The boy accepted the principle that he had to attend school. His adjustment also included the notion that he needn't exert himself. No one noticed for several years that his performance did not match his ability. Disappointment sometimes curbs the learning curve.

Boys Don't Cry

Tom was one of the better students in the fifth grade, but, on occasion, he would become so engrossed in something outside of school that his work would suffer.

When his dad brought home the puppy, Tom turned his attention and energy in the direction of his pet. He failed to do some important homework and test preparation. He was stunned to see a D on a test paper. The teacher expressed disappointment at his effort but observed that the best of people stumble at times. He liked that teacher.

Tom resolved to do better and quickly returned to his high-performance days. No more D's for him. The quality of his work improved to the point where the youngster wondered whether a B+ was a failure. His parents, knowing Tom was a very sensitive child, assured him that it wasn't necessary to earn all A's. They felt no anxiety about his academic life. He had learned from the puppy incident that his studies shouldn't be neglected, even when other exciting things were happening.

Then something not so pleasant occurred. Tom's class was selected to present a Thanksgiving Day play in the assembly. Tom and two others were to be American Indians. Of the three pupils, Tom was given the most lines. He spent several hours practicing by reading to his pet who listened intently each time as if she were evaluating his performance.

Halfway through the rehearsals the teacher suggested that the performers gather together the best costumes possible for their parts. Tom and the other two Indians should have head feathers and wrap themselves in Indian blankets.

"Where do I get an Indian blanket?" Tom inquired of his teacher.

The teacher, at the moment Tom asked the question, was busily reviewing a scene with three children and paid only offhand attention to Tom's query.

"Oh, ask your mother and if she can't get one, use any old blanket."

Tom's mother had no ready access to an Indian blanket, but when the child explained that any blanket would do, she set the issue aside. On the day of the play she produced an old baby blanket for Tom's use.

The group of excited young actors waited in the hall for their cue to enter the assembly room. Some reviewed their lines. Tom was ready.

"Tom! That's not an Indian blanket!" The dismay in the teacher's shriek penetrated Tom's skull and exploded in his brain like intersecting laser beams. He was simultaneously threatened and confused.

"But you said . . ."

The stage director's booming voice left Tom's protest unfinished.

"Okay. We're on. Let's go."

That evening, Tom's father conjectured that his son had been beaten up. "Maybe it was that new big kid that moved in around the corner."

"No. I don't think so," said his wife. "Look at his eyes. They're swollen. I think he's been crying—very long and very hard."

"I was not," disclaimed Tom after overhearing his mother's comment. "Never."

Tom then recounted the entire incident. He had been startled and upset by his teacher's sudden reversal. But the worst was yet to come.

The unnerved fifth-grader could remember none of his lines. He stood there, when it was time to speak, mute and helpless. No prompter had been appointed. Everything just stopped. The heroine of the play finally broke the tension by improvising some lines and moved the play forward.

The incident, trivial to some children, was almost traumatic to Tom. His self-esteem was shattered. He imagined himself being the focal point of his classmates' conversations as they laughingly told everyone of the episode.

The reality was quite different. The children in the play and in the audience quickly forgot the event. Tom should have also, but he didn't. He blamed his teacher for his embarrassment and, in turn, associated everything in school with his anguish. In a few days, the hurt lessened but some of the ill effects did not. He avoided future participation in school activities and displayed a somewhat diminished interest in everything academic. He no longer exhibited that bit of extra effort. Tom's grade average never regained its former level, but he did enter high school as a "B" student. Boys don't cry. Their mothers do.

Victims

In the story about seating charts and incorrectly recorded IQs, Fred Walters suffered the indignity of feeling belittled by his teacher. She had allowed an IQ score to set the level of a student's thinking. In the case of Fred, the score was an error, but he was, nevertheless, humiliated by the episode. He understood the denigration and so did his classmates. He watched as the teacher helped Joan organize an acceptable answer. She didn't do that for him. Why? She disliked him? How could she? She didn't know him. Maybe he was dumb. He saw her glance at the roll book. He had never considered himself stupid. He had, in fact, done quite well until now. But that work was all baby stuff. This was the sixth grade. Maybe he couldn't cut it up here.

Yet Fred isn't an underachiever. One embarrassing incident, unless particularly afflictive, usually doesn't shape a child's future. Unlike Tom, Fred quickly overcame his unpleasant experience.

Teachers can unwittingly contribute to the problems of students. They are in a high-pressure job with inadequate financial compensation. Teachers are "on-stage" when the class is present. All of the children in the class must be kept interested all of the time, every day. The teacher's personal problems cannot be brought to school. Elementary school teachers, in particular, face a constant audience of spirited, animated, vibrant children. Secondary school teachers are at war with adolescent hormones. Even the best teachers get rankled and thoughtlessly criticize a pupil.

Consider the following incident:

"Can anyone tell me," the teacher asks, "what would happen if I tried to mix water with oil?"

William raises his hand and is acknowledged by the teacher. With innocent seriousness, he responds, relying on an earlier misinterpretation, "The water would turn pink."

Thinking the boy was being flippant, the frustrated teacher responded, "Your brain would turn pink."

William stopped volunteering. The teacher should have corrected him with sensitivity, not rancor.

In another instance, Carolyn forgot her gym sneakers. The teacher assigned her a standing position in the back of the room for the entire session. For Carolyn, the experience was an assault on her ego. She never forgot her sneakers again—nor the teacher.

Occasionally, children will be punished for something they didn't do. Jill's teacher accused her of talking while the teacher was writing on the chalkboard. Her penalty was to write, "I must not talk without permission" 50 times. She protested. As a result, she was ordered to write it 100 times. The incident stayed on the top shelf of her brain's storage compartment.

Sometimes a teacher feels compelled to punish someone although the evidence is nonexistent. "Who broke the vase on my desk?" asks the third-grade teacher with a stern look. The class responds with stony silence. She repeats the question. More silence. Then, David fidgets. The teacher pounces. "David," she rules, "you sit close to my desk. You certainly look guilty. Stay after school today and we'll discuss your detention."

It doesn't happen that way? It sure does. "Innocent until proven guilty" is the axiom of the courts. Teachers often act on emotions. Accused and convicted of something he did not do, David remained suspicious and distrustful of teachers.

Sometimes, just an unwarranted comment from a teacher can turn off students. In one instance, a boy left his written assignment at home on the kitchen table. Rather than ask why the boy was unprepared, the teacher commented: "Rover ate it. Right, Jonathan?" The class chuckled. The teacher continued her verbal abuse on the hapless Jonathan: "Or did you leave it at home in the pocket of your other pants, the ones you were supposed to wear today?"

The class broke into open laughter. Jonathan was made to

look foolish in front of his peers. He didn't think much of education after that. He came to associate the school with ridicule and deprecated the value of learning.

Cindy, a bright underachiever, went to her teacher's desk to pick up an assignment. Just as she reached the desk, the teacher changed her mind. "I better give this to Marsha. Cindy, I have something easier for you." The thoughtless comment not only implied that Cindy was inferior but was heard by the class. To Cindy, the message was clear. The doubts she harbored about her ability were confirmed.

Teacher-pupil contacts are ongoing and teachers are not programmed robots. A parent cannot expect a human dealing with 20 to 30 children (more in some schools) for five hours, 186 days a year not to be abrasive with some child, sometime. Most parents would admit to a few intemperate remarks themselves with far less children. The reality and the statistics have little meaning for a sensitive child. A scathing remark, a frown, a disparaging gesture may injure a child's psyche. The undesired effect, if not reinforced, however, usually dissipates with time. Yet, many adults are able to recall a few vituperative remarks aimed at them by teachers. Sometimes the injury is lasting. Children face 11,000 hours of schooling. A disagreeable pupil-teacher contact cannot be ruled out.

Distasteful student-teacher contacts are part of the learning experience that prepares children for life and are only infrequently worrisome. A combination of negatives or a serious incident may have a lasting effect on even a normal child. Some teachers shouldn't be teachers, but that is true of all fields. Teachers, however, have tenure after two or three years and, short of a morals charge, can be removed only with extreme difficulty.

Sara had a misfit teacher at the wrong time. Mrs. K. had always been at least an average instructor who enjoyed working with children. A once very satisfactory marriage deteriorated and her instructional performance suffered accordingly. A teacher's personal problems should not affect her work at school, but in this case it did. The school principal was aware of Mrs. K.'s problem and tried to counsel her. Mrs. K. reached the point where, tiring of advice, she told the principal to "Mind your own damn business—I'm fine!" One day, perhaps near the edge, she wasn't so fine.

Sara, 11, had inherited her parents' features in a most appealing combination. The boys in the class teased her more than any other girl and Sara showed no sign of disliking the attention. On a given day, Mrs. K. called on Sara to read. Standing up, she noticed two classmates turned toward her making funny gestures. One blinked his eyes continuously and the other put his fingers into his ears. Sara giggled. Mrs. K.'s safety valve malfunctioned and the steam escaped.

The teacher's verbal onslaught pointed to Sara's lack of control, her ignorance, and her looks, which were certainly going to get her into trouble. While the tirade lasted less than a minute, Sara thought it endless. Mrs. K. regained control but couldn't justify her outburst. She compounded the injury by terminating the incident with "I've had enough of you. Sit down, stupid!"

The effect on Sara was lasting. Her work fell off in Mrs. K.'s class but the teacher, either feeling guilt or not wishing to have the episode reviewed, tended to give the girl higher marks than she earned.

Sara lost much of her interest in school and subconsciously limited her efforts. In the next semester she became a C student after a history of A's and B's. Her parents attributed her declining performance to a growing interest in boys.

The effects of experiences are usually cumulative, but sometimes even one can be a watershed. Negative experiences may be current, recent, or from the distant past. They may seem trivial to some, a natural part of life. In some fashion, they may have happened to many children without debilitating consequences. Sometimes they may have a profound, unfortunate effect on the child's image of himself and his attitude toward school.

Home and School Association

The experiences of a child at school and at home are usually quite different. An exception occurs when sibling comparisons are made. The Morgan girl in third grade was the fourth daughter of a striving, middle-class family. The parents were successful in providing models for their children. They worked hard, supported their church, loved their offspring, and cheated only a bit on their income tax. They considered teachers as royalty. Any complaint about behavior or poor work from the school would have been addressed immediately. They received no such complaints.

At one point in an assembly program, the principal rose to speak while the audience remained silent. The Morgan girl turned to a neighbor and whispered, too loudly, "I'll see you after school and tell you all about it." Her teacher, hearing the mini-disturbance, sprang to her feet. With an accusing finger pointing at the unlucky girl, and also too loudly, she warned "You be quiet!" As an afterthought, she added, "That's the first time I've ever had to reprimand a Morgan!"

Thinking her family might not survive the calamity, the eight-year-old sought out the teacher after the school day and apologized for her behavior. The adult, who had almost forgotten the incident, reassured the little girl that all was well. She certainly was excused.

At home, the child mentioned the incident, only to be confronted by her parents with a lecture about rudeness and inattention. Each member of the household, individually, was informed of the infraction. Mrs. Morgan, it seemed, excelled at inflating trivia into momentous problems. The child withdrew for months, but eventually dared to leave her shell. Her schoolwork, however, didn't return to normal.

The explanation became clear at a later time. The youngster had always been compared to her older sisters, but not favorably. Whatever she couldn't do, Doris could. Whatever she could do, Betsy could do better. At home, she was either an also-ran or a loser. In the episode reported, she had made up for her breach of the rules by voluntarily going to the teacher and apologizing. She wanted her mother to know she had handled the miscue herself and yearned for praise. To make the event more important, she exaggerated her offense. Her mother reacted accordingly and, as her final line, stated "Julia would never have done that."

Rivalry

Sibling rivalry exists without parents turning up the burner. Comparisons of offspring are inevitable, but should never, within hearing of the children, be negative. Inconsequential comments can turn off little children. "Mandy could read much better than Kim at her age. I guess Kim just won't be a good reader." Children try to play the roles assigned by parents. Kim might obligingly be a poor reader.

Brothers and sisters make their own comparisons, some of them farfetched and some accurate. Everything children hear and see affects their psyche to some degree. The adult may never know which barbs have stung and, in conjunction with others, have turned the child away from academics.

Differences

Nicole tells her own story. "I definitely went to school with a bad attitude. I was in a clique but I was different. My friends were small and cute. I was tall and awkward. I always had to stand in back of the line. I was the only girl in the fifth grade who wore a bra and the only girl in the clique who wore glasses. I used to cry after parties because I felt out of place. I was afraid to participate in class because I was so self-conscious. I so dreaded getting dressed for school each morning, I would make up excuses to stay at home."

The Nicoles in this world fail to reach their potential because of a physical characteristic which leaves them self-conscious. They can see themselves as too tall, too short, too heavy, or too clumsy. They have too much or too little. Something sets them off from their peers. They look for ways to adjust, to be one of the group.

"The only reason I was in the clique," said Nicole, "was because I'd dare to do crazy things like crawl up the aisle and tape 'kick me' signs on Joey Lingert's back."

Nicole says she can now talk of her experience without pain. "I guess Mom and Pop didn't realize what I was going through. I know I could have matched anyone in scholastics, but I didn't need anything else to set me apart. I just wanted to be one of the girls. Yes, I guess I was an underachieving child."

Nicole today is a fine, underachieving adult.

Andrew was a capable 10-year-old who happened to be the first one eliminated in a school spelling bee. The fates trampled on him again as he was the first one out in the next spelling contest. He wasn't a poor speller. By chance, he was given words he could not handle. Andrew lost confidence. He became nervous when the teacher arranged another spelling match, and by the time it was his turn, blurted out anything just to get it over with. The teacher paid no heed to such minutiae. Andrew saw it differently. He avoided nonwritten competitive activities in the future even when he could have performed well.

Friends

Brian was a bright, healthy boy with many friends, a variety of interests and an excellent record in school. He announced after his eleventh birthday that he was going to be an astronomer.

"His father and I thought that was a respected profession but rather limited in terms of income," his mother remembered. "We weren't opposed to his choice. We just thought he was capable of doing something more financially rewarding— perhaps law or medicine or business. Anyway, we knew that he might change his mind several times over and voiced no objection."

Then something happened. His mother recalled an incident which occurred at that time. Brian and his pal, Mike, burst through the kitchen door as excited as two boys can get. They were trying to listen to each other, but neither could suppress his compulsive desire to talk. They left the kitchen, tongues wagging simultaneously.

"Mom," Brian yelled at his mother, "Mike and me are going to use the extension upstairs. Don't touch the phone down here. Okay? Please!"

After the incident, things were never the same again. Brian changed. It was as if some loved one died or he had contracted a serious disease. The bubbling, enthusiastic almost-teenager suddenly became solemn and withdrawn. His life balloon was punctured.

"Brian's father and I tried talking to him but he denied that anything was wrong. Gradually Brian spent more time at home. His friends called for a while but he usually didn't answer them. Eventually, the calls stopped. Brian rarely went out anymore. He was in his room most of the time. His grades plummeted.

"We never heard what happened from Brian. We noticed that Mike didn't come around anymore, so one day I called his home and spoke to his mother. There had been no argument. He told me that Brian and he had been invited to join a boys' club in the neighborhood. The club called itself the 'Smart Group' and the members were known as 'Smarts.' They had white and gray sweaters with the drawing of a human brain as the emblem.

"The kids considered it an honor to belong and, although it wasn't the kind of organization I approved of, I never had a voice in it. Mike was accepted but Brian was blackballed. Mike said they didn't give Brian any reason. They invited him to join and when he agreed, they rejected him. How could these boys have been so cruel?"

Brian was unprepared to cope with a setback of this dimension. He wasn't the only one invited and turned down. The other children were hurt or angry but Brian's life was changed.

Wrap-Up

Negative experiences occur in many varieties and combinations. A capricious fate determines the number and extent of happenings that affect children adversely. Parents cannot shelter their children from unfortunate incidents and frequently have no knowledge of these events. Sometimes parents themselves cause the event.

The negative effects may be the result of pupil-teacher interaction, sibling comparisons and rivalry, peer exclusion, or an almost innumerable number of possible categories.

A child may:

- Do something foolish in school and be laughed at by his classmates
- Be caught doing something wrong, including a first-time mistake

- Be embarrassed by parental actions when visiting the school or elsewhere
- Be punished unreasonably for poor schoolwork
- Be forced to perform some school-type talent in front of adults without preparation
- Develop feelings of guilt associated with poor performance
- Lose confidence because of earlier failure
- Experience a setback without a subsequent success
- Become the butt of a joke or prank by classmates

Negative experiences, singly or in combination, may dampen your child's enthusiasm for school. Your task is to establish a close rapport with the youngster so that he may be willing to discuss these unfavorable incidents with you.

The prescriptive chapters will delineate the measures you may employ which include the vital strengthening of your child's self-esteem.

7

Is Your Child a Bit Different?

The Late Arrivers

Both of Allen's parents are successful in their careers. His mother, despite some misgivings on the part of her superiors, has combined native ability, training, and drive to penetrate the upper echelon of corporate management. Her husband has established his own expanding accounting firm. Both parents are still in their 30s. Their first child, Joanna, now nine and in the fourth grade, has overcome some early childhood illnesses. Her health is now satisfactory, she excels in school, and is a happy child. The problem at the moment is their perception of Allen.

The seven-year-old second-grader has escaped his sister's early childhood illnesses, but his school progress is worrisome. The child's physical growth has been normal but his intellect appears sluggish. He does everything his contemporaries do but never well. He enjoys toys but doesn't manipulate them. He plays games but seems disinterested. He shows little desire to win. He laughs frequently, perhaps too much. When Joanna is home, everyone is aware of her. She moves, talks, and acts. Allen is quiet and disturbs no one. Frequently, he just sits and watches. His mother notes, "He's just an observer, I guess, not a participant." Nonetheless, both parents are quite concerned. Could there be a developmental disorder in their child?

Allen's teacher graciously agrees to meet with her on Wednesday after dismissal time. Allen's mother, despite deadlines at work, takes time off to visit the school.

As the teacher reviews Allen's record from kindergarten to the moment, the parent interrupts. "Yes. I know all that. I don't mean to be rude but I want to get right to the issue. He doesn't do things like he should. Is there something wrong with him?"

The teacher's countenance reveals surprise.

"I know of nothing wrong. He's just slow . . ."

"He's retarded? No! He can't be!"

"I didn't mean to upset you," she apologizes. "I was going to say he is slow in developing. All the tests show he's above average in ability. He's just immature. Believe me. There's nothing wrong with Allen."

There was nothing wrong with Allen. The teacher was justifiably unconcerned. There were no confirming signs of any mental disability. The numbers substantiated the child's normalcy. In a group of typical children, about two-thirds, more or less, follow the prescribed developmental charts. About a sixth of the group accelerate and about another sixth fall behind. Allen was bringing up the rear of the bottom segment but was still safely within the acceptable range. Bright children tend, based on statistical measures, to develop quickly both mentally and physically. There are always exceptions. Allen was an exception.

Developmental characteristics may not be exactly uniform. A child may be advanced in some areas, such as speaking ability, but be hampered by lagging development in writing skills. As long as none of the areas imply an impairment, there should be no concern. If some aspects are severely depressed, as revealed by testing, a psychologist may suspect and test for minimal cerebral dysfunction.

The rate of development in children varies. Educators use the term "readiness," referred to in the last chapter, to indicate whether a child has reached the mental and physiological state at which he can learn a subject without undue stress. Forcing him to learn or attempt to learn when he hasn't reached an appropriate developmental level may be damaging. The resulting frustration may turn the child against learning that topic later when he is ready. The experience may then be classified as negative.

The growth stages of all children are the same but children reach them at different times. Allen will catch up. Until he does, his parents, no matter how reassured, will worry. But that's a characteristic of parents.

Some children, with all of their developmental skills at the proper level, nevertheless tend to plow along in school without demonstrating their innate possibilities. Then something happens. They change suddenly and dramatically. Their work levels move into high gear.

Bob, who was just above the middle of his class in elementary school, became an outstanding student at the secondary level. Ann, whose grades rose and fell depending on her interests at the time, became a top student in her senior year in high school. Once in college, she continued on until she had earned a doctorate. George, a C+ to B− student, seemed satisfied with a high school diploma. After trying several jobs over a three-year span, he enrolled in college. Eight years later he accepted a medical residency at a large teaching hospital.

Known as the "quiet kid," Ed attracted little attention. His mother observed that although Ed had playmates, they always came to him. Sometimes they stopped at the house and asked him to come out. He usually did. At other times, he declined. He had something else to do. The something else was neither a household chore nor schoolwork. Ed spent many hours in his bedroom or reading in the living room.

The youngster enjoyed receiving and opening gifts but never showed childish excitement, even at Christmas time. He listened intently to family, especially adult conversations, but rarely volunteered anything. He helped his two younger brothers dress or find a toy but didn't play with them. He did all right in school but his parents felt he could do better. He was rarely in any kind of difficulty in school or at home.

Both parents tried at times to provide quality time for Ed. Together and individually, they engaged him in direct conversation. They asked him about himself, his interests, his desires. They spoke to him one-on-one. Ed's replies were almost always laconic. He revealed little. Yet, he showed no signs of resentment. He didn't make demands or complain. He seemed happy enough, but some essential spark was missing.

Any medical or psychological diagnosis would have established nothing. Ed was one of those not-too-uncommon people known as late bloomers who, seemingly from nowhere, burst onto the scene. One spring, Ed was a docile, unassuming elementary schoolchild. Then he emerged from a typical summer vacation into a high-spirited, driving secondary school freshman. In his senior year, he was voted the most likely to succeed. Ed's development lagged behind his peers, but when he did blossom, he led the pack.

Nature Changed the Die

Marty was a puzzle to his parents and his teachers. He was quite intelligent, as indicated by the numbers and other evaluations. Sometimes his work was outstanding. More often, it was average. He was consistent in his inconsistency from first to twelfth grade. Like a sun flare, he suddenly rose to great heights, only to fall back again to mediocrity.

Sometimes his mother worried because, as noted, parents do that well. She tried to analyze him. He had no friends, she thought, but many friendly acquaintances. Marty shunned extracurricular activities in school, belonged to no clubs, and avoided athletics. When he had free time, he left the house, usually on his bike, and went somewhere. She never was sure where. He was home on time for dinner, did his homework without help, watched some television, and went to bed. He seemed perfectly content with life.

Nothing was wrong with Marty. He was, by nature, a loner. His achievement level could have been raised somewhat by helping him to understand himself, society, and how he fit into it. Such understandings should have started in elementary school so that Marty could have learned to adjust to situations he confronted.

Paul's mother knew at a very early age he was an outside person. He played in front of the house, the sides, or the back, but not inside. Daylight meant outside. Weather meant nothing. He liked the sunshine but thought rain wasn't too bad either. Snow was a joy. Temperature extremes merely dictated the kind of outerwear. In the child's eyes, all weather meant fun time.

The pavement was good for trike-riding, but grass was great for running, tumbling, and digging. Flowers were beautiful, insects were unimportant, and worms were interesting.

Wind sometimes was annoying because it pushed his little frame around and scattered his belongings. But he was getting bigger and stronger every day and faced the challenge with confidence.

When darkness took over, he played in the house, running his motor at full speed. One activity followed another without a break. He never slowed down. At some point in the evening he just stopped. His mother would find him, asleep, on a chair, a sofa, or stretched out on a rug. She learned to bathe him early in the evening.

The day came for Paul to start school. His mother thought kindergarten might be a problem; it wasn't. Paul adapted quickly, made new friends, and thought the one-half day spent at the nearby school acceptable. First grade was another matter. Paul came home for lunch on the third day and announced that he wasn't returning that afternoon. He explained to his questioning mother that the morning was enough; he didn't like or need the afternoon. The outside kid, in his way, was offering a compromise. He would attend school for half a day. No more.

Although Paul couldn't win this argument, he became a classic underachiever. Weekends and holidays were blessings. School days were irksome. He resented learning anything which, in his view, was unappealing or useless. Paul read well at home but didn't for the teacher. In school, arithmetic had no purpose, but at home he understood money and could count or apportion it accurately. Nature and science captured and held his attention. Gymnastics were fine.

By the third grade, Paul's attraction to everything associated with school had waned. He became neutral even about his former favorite topics and, despite measures from encouragement to punishment, his parents could not generate interest in school.

"He needs subjects that appeal to him," the counselor advised the parents. "What really excites him?"

"Let's see," said Paul's father. "He likes fishing, boating, and swimming."

These subjects were not being offered by Paul's elementary school that year.

Paul and the many thousands like him dislike school but nothing the school does causes the problem. Schools provide a curriculum suitable for most children as decreed by society. Paul didn't fit the common mold. He was a bit different. He might have done well with an Aristotle-type teacher under a tree, but couldn't adjust to a conventional teacher under a roof.

Some children, healthy from a psychological view, digress from the majority in preferences and interests. No statistics exist to cover this group. Few if any educators write about them. However, they're there and will appear again in future generations.

Differences have their incubation periods in childhood. Some of these nonconformities are not conducive to academic learning. They should be dealt with in a realistic and practical manner when the child is young. Differences in children's styles must be examined intelligently. Not everything lends itself to change. For instance, attempts to make left-handed children into right-handers not only fail but, in some cases, can cause unhealthy outcomes. The correct procedure is to identify the dissimilarities and have the child understand them. Left-handed people today have learned to live in a right-handed world. They can drive right-handed automobiles and operate right-handed slot machines.

There are no limits to the variations in people. Some examples are people who:

- Prefer staying up and working at night
- Must be outdoors to be productive
- Can't enjoy being spectators or part of an audience but must be actively involved
- Can perform satisfactorily only when alone

Wrap-Up

Normal young children sometimes fall behind in a given growth area without cause for worry. For instance, a child may reverse letters in first grade, but the condition may correct itself by the time he is seven. He may require more time than most to develop good eye-hand coordination, but by the time he's eight, his parents will probably have already forgotten their concern.

Children march to many different drummers without being intellectually enervated. *If their individual urges clash with the arrangement of the school, they may become educationally debilitated unless someone, such as a parent, intervenes.*

8

A Child Too Bright
A Tale of Two Citizens

The Fifties

Jerome and Stanton were childhood buddies. Jerome had been a loner and Stanton was a new kid in the school when the two became classmates in the sixth grade. As the months went on, they "found" each other.

Each had a color for a surname. Jerome insisted that his given name never be abbreviated. He wasn't Jer or Jerry to peers, teachers, parents. He was Jerome. Stanton didn't care about shortening his own name. He answered to Stan or anything else that wasn't insulting. Jerome had, he thought, some profound, albeit esoteric reason for refusing to be called anything less than his full name. A month later, overwhelmed by curiosity, he asked for an explanation. There was no mystery. Jerome had a cousin, Geraldine, who was called Gerri. He didn't want a girl's name.

Their friendship had begun as they realized a line of private communication was developing between them. Neither one was particularly attentive in class and both experienced the explosive awakening from a reverie when the annoyed teacher, noticing their glazed eyes, called on them rather sharply.

"Jerome!"

"I'm sorry. I wasn't listening."

"Stan. Repeat my question."

"I'm really sorry too. I didn't hear you."

"You two had better stay wide-awake. That's the only way you'll get promoted."

Both boys nodded in agreement but, as they glanced at each other, their eye movements exchanged a message. No way. This was a "no effort necessary" class. It was going to be a long dull year. Neither boy was concerned about the teacher's warning. Neither believed the threat, nor cared.

As the school term aged, the boys polished their unspoken communication. They were becoming proficient in an area usually reserved for females. They could send messages to each other by shifting their eyes slightly, raising an eyebrow, or tilting their heads. They learned to send signals without written or spoken words.

Both children remembered the very day they progressed from friendly to friendship. The teacher was speaking.

"Here in this area," she said, as her hand circled the large wall map, "the people have Asiatic features. Now, over here, in the subcontinent we call India, the inhabitants do not have Oriental features. They are dark-skinned. As we move westward, we find Caucasian or white people. What is it, Stan?"

"Anthropologists consider most of the people in India to be Caucasian because . . ."

"No, Stan. Please. You're not right."

"But I am."

"Then maybe you ought to write a book."

The class laughed. Stan glanced at Jerome and detected an almost imperceptible smile. Jerome's eyes flashed a silent message of encouragement. Stay with it.

"The east Indian language is part of the Indo-European family," the determined, and now supported, Stan shot back.

The teacher terminated the assault on her accuracy.

"We're not studying anthropology or philosophy and we're not racists. We don't care what the people are.

We're studying geography. You're just delaying the lesson. Let's go on.''

Stan looked at Jerome, expecting a hint of a smirk, but Jerome was smiling broadly.

As the class was leaving for lunch, Jerome caught up to Stan. ''Hey, Stanton. I've got some charcoal, potassium nitrate, and sulfur in my basement. Want to come over after school?''

''Gunpowder!'' Stan exclaimed and then imitated an explosive sound.

''Sure, I'll be over.''

The friendship lasted for years.

One Friday, the teacher had four questions ready for their ''fun time.'' Rather than have uninterrupted instruction, she frequently provided a few stimulating minutes between subjects as a change of pace. She would read to the class, have them stand and stretch, or ask some interesting questions. Her favorite exercise was the questions.

''Remember, raise your hand and don't call out. First, I'll give you all the questions. Then I'll ask them one at a time. Think them through before raising your hand. Ready?

''All right. The lion tamer and the child returned to their trailer. The child was the son of the lion tamer, but the lion tamer wasn't the father of the child. Explain.

''Next question. What do doctors consider most injurious to the lungs?

''Okay. Let's try some arithmetic. How many quarters of a quarter are there in half of a half?

''Finally. Here's one from science. There's a lot of talk about the possibility of life on Mars, but science has *proved* that one planet in our solar system does, in fact, have life. Which one?''

Hands jumped toward the ceiling all over the room. The teacher allowed some extra thinking time and was about to call on Tony when she noticed a disinterested Jerome reading a paperback. She was annoyed.

''Jerry!'' she snapped.

No response.

''Jerome! Give me an answer.''

Without taking his eyes off the page the youngster, in a well-modulated voice, said, "His mother, dust, four, and earth."

All hands went down.

She did not call on him for the balance of the semester and he did not volunteer any information.

The Sixties

The administrator was trying to straighten out the confusing episode. "Now, Mr. Green . . ."

"Jerome is good enough," the young man offered.

"Whatever. Jerome, Professor Dodd has sent me your exam paper and the textbook. Your answer on Kipling is the same as the book's. Not the same content. The same words! Look at this, line for line. Even the commas are in the same place."

"So? He asked the question that was in the book so I gave just what the book said."

"That's not the issue. You couldn't have repeated the text of the book *exactly* unless you were looking at it during the test. Right?"

"No. I didn't have the book with me. I answered from memory."

The dean was becoming exasperated. "Are you saying, sir, that you have a photographic memory?"

"I don't call it anything. The page answered the question so I used it. I don't see anything wrong."

"I don't either if you truly can recall every detail of what you read. Now, let's find out. I'll give you an article to read, say, any one over there on the shelf, and then ask you to write out one of the pages. If you can, or even come close, I'll just drop the matter. Fair?"

"No. I don't have to prove anything."

"Mr. Green, or Jerome. You've been accused of cheating. If you want to stay in this college, you've got two choices. Either prove the remarkable recall power you claim or admit you did something wrong. If you give such an admission, you'll fail the course but can continue with your studies. It's one or the other. If neither, you'll be expelled.''

"I'll accept your article memory test on one condition. When I prove I'm right, you fire Professor Dodd or any other professor who asks questions right out of the book. I can stay home and read books."

The administrator could not believe the effrontery of this student. Jerome could no longer attend this college.

The training battalion stood on the parade grounds, almost a thousand in number. The first sergeant, in his best mangled English, yelled, "Towel-yon, tench hut!"

Almost a thousand young people responded, making a cracking sound as their shoes met at the heel.

"'Port!" bellowed the sergeant.

Each company leader shouted in turn.

"All prec count fer!"

Satisfied, the first sergeant turned to the battalion commander ready to report that all of them were present and accounted for when a loud laugh punctured the stillness. The men in Jerome's platoon stifled their urge to follow his lead. They knew better. Jerome had done it again. "What," he later explained to the captain, "could be more humorous than a thousand grown men lining up like toy soldiers?"

"Perhaps," said the officer, "some company punishment could be funnier."

After two weeks of spending his spare time cleaning the kitchen, Jerome had a night off. Together with his only army friend, he was walking in the middle of the road that led to the post exchange. A jeep bearing the insignia of the military police was approaching, going the wrong way on the one-way road. The soldiers, walking along, moved to the sides to let the vehicle pass. All except one.

The audience applauded as the college president read the names of the graduating students.

"Next, graduating summa cum laude, is Brown, Stanton M."

The Seventies

The new president of the corporation swung his chair away from the window to face his intercom. "Yes?" he asked the box. The box answered. "I've got the folders of those applicants you wanted for the chief-of-operations opening. Three good possibilities and this other . . . guy."

"What other guy?"

"I'm just not sure of this fellow, Mr. Brown. He's just a clerk in our warehouse. No degree or anything. Yet, he comes highly recommended."

"Well, include his folder with the others. I'll look it over later."

"One more thing, sir. This guy wrote on his application that he's in charge of something I never heard of. I can't find it in any inventory. Very strange."

"Like what?"

"Well, he wrote that he's an expert in ordering wood-encased, manually operated, multilingual data recorders with attached correctors."

"I never heard of it either. Check IBM's catalog. If it's not in there, forget it."

Stanton swung his chair back to the window. "Lots of roofs out there," he told himself. Then another thought. "I think I'm going to love this job. What a challenge.

"Pencils!" his voice thundered as a thought struck him. "Multi . . . data recorder . . . with erasers!"

He swung back to his intercom almost too fast and grabbed the desk to slow down.

"Johnson."

"He just left for a break, sir. Can I help you?"

"Yes, Liz. There's a fellow over in warehousing I want to see. Right now. His name is Jerome Green."

Wrap-Up

The fortunes of Jerome and Stanton are continued in a later chapter with some insight into their motivations and reactions. American schools, spurred on by Soviet space competition in the 1960s, made efforts to advance American talents and devised specialized programs for gifted children. Today, few districts exist that offer nothing for the needs of mentally superior youngsters. However, a problem still exists for a number of these children who have not adjusted to society. Your youngster may be one of this group—a child too bright.

9

The Divergent-Thinking Child

The Misfit

The administrator in the Fort Huron public school is proud of his position and usually enjoys each working day. He gains a great deal of satisfaction from helping children grow into fine, well-educated citizens. But, he reminds himself, not every day can be pleasant. Difficult tasks are sometimes unavoidable. Today, for instance, he has to tell Tommy's mother about the decision of the school board.

Tommy is a nice child. He doesn't start fights, disrupt the class, or back-talk his teacher. In fact, in his own way, the boy is respectful toward adults. But that is the problem. "In his own way." Tommy is just strange. He frequently gazes through the window oblivious to everything in the classroom. His attention can easily be captured by a robin devouring a worm or the windblown journey of an autumn leaf.

Tommy is polite, but he challenges explanations. The fact that these assertions came from authorities such as textbook writers doesn't impress him. Tommy wants proof. There isn't evidence readily available for everything. A teacher at times must rely on statements such as "Because I say so" or "That's the way it's always been done." Tommy finds such clarifications unacceptable. Even when he says nothing, his face registers disbelief.

Besides, Tommy is odd in other ways, muses the administrator. The child has his own peculiar brand of humor. He laughs at matters others consider somber. He thinks lining up by size at the sound of the school bell is funny. And worse, he wants to follow his own compulsions, irrespective of the teacher's plans.

Awkward and burdened by a hearing problem, Tommy does not compete in the usual children's games on the school playground. He has few friends and is taunted frequently. However, his hearing loss is not the major concern. The problem, the administrator is convinced, is the youngster's inability to think properly.

This is not the first time, the administrator knows, young Tom has run into educational problems. Earlier, in his first school near Fort Gratiot, where the discipline is very severe, the lad had rebelled and run away.

"Well, Tommy will probably grow up to be one of those nonachievers, one of those people who are decent but unreliable. He'll probably be . . . ." The knock on the door interrupts the administrator's flow of thought. He looks up and forces a smile. Tommy's mother, having been summoned, is standing just outside of the office, wearing an immobile poignant expression. Telling this unfortunate woman that her boy doesn't belong with normal children is a vexatious but necessary chore. Parents never readily accept the failure of their child and sometimes aren't very gracious when told.

He would soften the blow as well as he could. He would counsel the mother on how the boy should be raised: strict adherence to rules, continuous discipline, and acceptance of established procedures. He would try to impress upon her the nature of the lad's limitations.

"Please. Please. Come right in. How are you today, Mrs. Edison? Here, sit on this chair. I'm glad you were able to come. I have some important things to tell you."

Sometimes you shouldn't listen. Tom's parents didn't.

High Divergency

There are people with highly divergent potential. They are the discoverers of fire and inventors of the wheel. They are frequently misunderstood and their contributions accepted only belatedly. They often incur the wrath of the vested interests of their time. Too often, their kind is burned at the stake or broken on the rack. Galileo Galilei was forced to confess that he didn't see what he saw in the macrocosm of physical science. Louis Pasteur was held in contempt for his understanding of the microcosm of biological science.

All of these people, past and present, possess an unusual aspect of intellect, one that can't be determined in the prescribed fashion, a mysterious type of acumen—a creative intelligence.

In this work, creative thinking is equated with divergent intelligence. The creative child may be described as one who does more self-generating cognition, more independent thinking than his peers. His overt behavior can be observed and evaluated, but it may be extremely difficult to unscramble his reasoning process. His progress in school may be a poor barometer of his adjustment in the nonscholastic world. *In school, he may be considered an underachiever.*

Such children, because of their nontypical interpretations of the scene about them, and their unusual actions and reactions, may be subjected to criticism and derision. Many react by stifling their creativity, learning to drift with the conventional tide. A few stay with their innate bent, and a few of these become famous adults.

There are no statistics on underachievers who are divergent thinkers. Many students, arrested in the C+ to B– level when they should surpass the group, might fit into this category.

The divergent thinker may escape identification since all normal people have a degree of creative intelligence. As a parent, you should watch for certain traits which are sometimes profound, but sometimes ephemeral. Your underachieving offspring may just be one of those unusual kids with elevated divergent capability. Here are some helpful clues based on the

characteristics of identified creative youngsters. Do they remind you of your child?

She's Doing What?

The creative youngster may be nonconformist in thought and
private actions, although these urges are often suppressed. Pat,
a young girl of 13, asked for and received an electric race car
set for Christmas. The excitement of watching the toy cars
speed around the track intrigued her. When Pat's girlfriends
came to her house the cars disappeared and more conventional
props materialized. A hard-rock tape was turned on. Color
photos of TV stars and red sports cars were produced. The
young girl feared her peers would be disturbed by her unor-
thodox interest. Pat forced herself to be like the others. Her fear
of disapproval revised her thinking. By covering up her true
desires Pat was able to fit in with the mainstream.

Use Your Imagination!

Imagination is alive and well in the mind of the creative
child. He needs no encouragement. He uses this remarkable
force to keep himself occupied, from inventing games to
conceptualizing full-scale events. Two such children formed
a partnership imitating an adult enterprise. Jill and Beth
collaborated in a weekly publication called "Kidstuff." The
enterprising preadolescent journalists ran the operation themselves, in their own way. Their "editorials" reflected their own
views which differed not only from those of adults, but from
the outlook of their friends.

The creative gift cannot be consumed. Creative children
form original ideas as a matter of course. They discover
concepts without realizing they've done so. They encounter
creative surges without conscious thought. Jill and Beth had
silent partners—their imaginations.

What If . . .

Creative children like problems with more than one possible solution. Answers to their questions are numerous since they see multiple possibilities and consequences. They see many right ways to do things.

Creative youngsters are also attracted to "What if . . ." problems, including those that have no certain answers. What if George Washington had been born a girl? Would the United States have gained its independence? What would the world be like today? What if the world suddenly ran out of oil? What would happen to civilization? What if people stopped getting older? What would happen to the population and the resources of the earth?

He's in His Room . . . Writing a Poem

One clue that a child possesses high creativity may be found in his desire to write. Creative children may begin writing diaries and letters or even short stories at an early age. They may write poetry. Writing provides a boundless outlet for unsuppressible imaginations.

Jill and Beth created a "Poetry Page" with the contributions made solely by the two of them. Although their works were not professional, the effort permitted a flowering of creativity.

There's Nothing Wrong with Him: It's His Hobby

Children with divergent intelligence often have hobbies based on their imaginations. They may have sampled some field of learning in school, latched onto a fragment from television or followed through on an intriguing idea they heard about. A particular pursuit, however, may have no relationship to school studies or parent-directed activities. The child makes the selection with the help of that silent partner. The parents can only marvel at what unfolds.

Richard became fascinated with ancient Egypt and, with the help of library books and clay, built a valley of pyramids and a sphinx. His parents offered encouragement, which he didn't need, and constructive advice, which he ignored. His play area in the basement became a model of ancient Egyptian architecture.

One day the parents, as they had done before, escorted some friends to the building area to display, proudly, their son's talent. To their dismay, they found the site had undergone demolition.

"What happened?" the father queried the boy.

"Oh, it wasn't any good so I crushed it."

"Why wasn't it 'any good'?"

"The buildings weren't in proportion," explained the seven-year-old to the astonished parents.

It'll Never Get Off the Ground

Creative children and adults have the ability to combine the incongruous and create something unique. They may have been the first ones to bring together the unlikely combination of peanut butter and jelly in a sandwich. Once accepted, their ideas become commonplace, and no one pauses to consider the original source. Initially, the idea of divergent thinkers have to overcome the traditional minds that invariably proclaim "If it's any good, why hasn't someone done it before?" or "It's just a fad. It'll pass."

I See Problems Ahead

Divergent thinkers may see a problem unfolding before it is generally recognized.

A group of boys belonged to a club which met each Friday evening. All of the children enjoyed the organization and looked forward to planning sporting events and parties. One serious difficulty was the inability of any president to keep order during the meetings. Many approaches were tried but all failed. Finally, one member suggested that fines be levied against the unruly. After some discussion, the majority agreed.

"It won't work. In fact, it'll break us up," protested a lonely dissenter. The boy was voted down and the system was instituted. As predicted, the fines caused arguments and irritations and in one raucous meeting, a large group of boys walked out. The club was dismantled.

A bank brought in a group of efficiency experts to find ways to reduce operational costs. The strategists changed some operating systems, reduced personnel, collected their fees and went to another bank.

"It won't work," commented one employee, the same divergent thinker, now grown. "These people are outsiders. They don't have a feel for our situation."

Some of his fellow employees viewed the young man with disdain. He'd been there only one year and already felt qualified to disagree with skilled professional personnel. His advice went unheeded.

The new economies did fail. Capable and experienced workers, under pressure because of staff shortages, left. Unhappy customers, confronting unfamiliar systems and replacement personnel, took their accounts elsewhere.

The divergent thinker was not clairvoyant. He was able to understand the consequences of the changes by perceiving and combining more essential elements than had been used by the efficiency experts. The management team that had launched the cost-cutting programs faced a diminished bottom line. They reacted by discharging some of the lower-echelon personnel, including the divergent thinker.

The Big Questions

Most children are not overly concerned with the meaning of life, but the divergent thinker may be. He may ponder this complexity, even at a young age. He is able to examine the larger picture due to his inventive, ever-expanding interests. He may ask disturbing questions for a youngster such as, "If God created the universe, who created God?"

The divergent thinker considers problems that have no direct effect on him, considerations most children leave to adults. He worries—sometimes more than his parents realize—about starving Africans, overpopulation, and the environment.

The creative child is compassionate. He is able to feel deep sorrow for someone wronged. He may sense the true plight of an individual or a cause. He wants to know why bad things happen.

His Mind Is All Over the Place

Divergent intelligence is flexible. Because his mind resists being bound, the child's limitations are few. Lack of strict boundaries allows him to move from one thought to another or from one activity to another. His flexibility lubricates his thinking, which never becomes stale.

He's in His Own World

Understandably, the creative child is a fervent daydreamer. Reality is often too oppressive or confining for his free-spirited thinking. He lets his mind soar. He may remain a dreamer or create a theory that will attract global attention. His growth depends on experience and much of that depends on his parents.

Wrap-Up

Standard intelligence tests measure creativity inadequately or not at all. Creativity is an integral part of intelligence, nevertheless, and draws for its fulfillment on all other intellectual components. People with the most developed divergent intelligence usually have above-average IQs but are not necessarily near the top of the scale.

Creative ideas may not be useful at their birth; it may take years or decades—even centuries—for them to be recognized. The creative thinker may foresee problems not yet ripe and dangers still obscure. He may offer solutions that others consider unnecessary and may pursue goals whose utility is not yet understood. He frequently encounters a wall of resistance and may not always persevere. As Albert Einstein observed: "Against every great and noble endeavor stands a million mediocre minds." The creative person sometimes becomes a victim of his own originality. He may become an outcast.

You should remember this:

All children exhibit some creativity and some creative moments. One characteristic, one incident, or one response with the flavor of divergent thinking is not sufficient to draw a conclusion. The child should be evaluated carefully over time—by you.

If you tell the child's teachers or other school personnel your child is a divergent thinker, they may not understand. They'll know the words "divergent" and "creative," but they may not be able to relate these to the youngster's performance and behavior. Even if they did, they might have no way of dealing with it.

Then what? Your task need not be impossible, frustrating, or difficult. Utilize the general remedial approach in Part III of this volume and read the specifics on handling a young divergent thinker.

The combination of his various intellectual abilities will determine his potential. Tommy's parents rejected the advice of the school administrator and nurtured their son's unique capacities. They bought him books and laboratory equipment and encouraged him to read and experiment. He pursued his own interests and, with their assistance, found answers to the questions he himself posed. He did that all his life.

Thomas Alva Edison was always aware that he was "different," but he learned to fit into society as it existed without curtailing the expression of his inventive genius.

If your child is an underachiever because he perceives the world in his own inimitable way, your obligation is to have him:

- Understand himself and his talents
- Become an academic achiever
- Advance his own career in a world of convergent thinkers

PART III
THE REMEDIAL PROCESS

10

Getting Started

Underachievement is a symptom of a learning weakness, not a disability in and of itself. As I mentioned earlier, there are many possible causes for underachievement. If you know the cause or causes, you're a step ahead in the remediation process. You may omit techniques that are unnecessary for helping your child and focus only on his particular needs. More than likely, although you may have a suspicion or two, you are probably not at all certain of the source of the problem.

You have little to lose by applying the comprehensive prescriptive program to follow. My view is that virtually every elementary school child would benefit from an appropriate version of the system. Even achievers can be improved. There is nothing intrinsically wrong with becoming a winner.

All parents sending a child to elementary school should ask themselves some important questions about the education of their youngster.

- Will my child receive all the opportunities and experiences necessary for full intellectual development in a reasonable and timely fashion?
- Could some specific aspect of my child's faculties be sharpened and elevated to a more desirable level?
- Could some latent talent of my child be enhanced by a special identification and enrichment program?

- Can the effects of some cognitive weakness in my child be ameliorated by timely intervention?
- Is it possible that some creative gift in my child lies moribund because it lacks recognition, understanding, and stimulation?

Parents should oversee their child's total education, cooperate with the school, and support efforts to strengthen curricula. At home, the parents should provide the vital learning opportunities that the schools omit, but ones which will harmonize with the formal education of the school.

Many children are *borderline* underachievers and therefore difficult to classify. Their measured intelligence suggests that they should be doing better academically, but they are not substantially below their potential. Schools rarely are concerned about them. Administrators have more pressing problems requiring immediate attention. Teachers are awash in daily duties. Each child, performing below his innate capacity, is just another insignificant statistic in the educational system—except to that child's parents.

The sales pitch of the U.S. Army recruiter is quite appropriate for these children. "Be all you can be." Students should strive toward the higher side of their potential. Parents should see that they get there.

This prescriptive program is designed to arrest any decline in progress and then raise the performance level of the underachiever.

The techniques involved require no formal training, no specialized abilities, and no specific textbooks. This program is based on over 30 years of experience in teaching students from preschool through college and instructing and supervising teachers. It is based on my attempt to bridge the gap between psychological theories of learning and practical education.

Thoughts That Affect Your Performance

1. Every family has a member who is the "expert on all things," a maven, one of the cognoscenti, who is sure to have an opinion on how well you're bringing up your children. Heed your own counsel. You know your own kid best.

2. This is a book of suggested procedures. Just as every child is an individual, so is his parent. Feel free to modify any of the recommendations.

3. Don't wait to get started. There is no makeup formula to replace lost childhood years or days. Certainly, your child might turn himself around, but how much and when? Based on the state of American education today, the cavalry isn't coming. You'll have to accept the challenge yourself.

4. Be cautious about easy remedies. Examine all such approaches carefully. A good tutor may be helpful in raising a specific subject grade, but the fundamentals of your child's learning pattern may not be altered.

5. No time limit is applicable to the success of this program. Improvements may be slow or rapid. Sometimes the segments will seem to have no effect and then, suddenly, they coalesce. The child, all at once, will understand. The last straw, instead of breaking the camel's back, provides the insight.

6. Never overlook the primary goal of the program, a frequent error. You want your child to master the fundamentals of learning which will then become applicable to every learning-type situation he will encounter in and out of school. Elementary schools are properly named; they are the schools that teach the basics, or should.

7. You will be utilizing a multifaceted approach which has already been prepared for you. All you need to do is follow the directions delineated. Through an intricate weaving pattern built into the program, you will be combining the cognitive and affective (emotional) sides of learning and coordinating your efforts at home with the instruction at school.

8. Forget formal sessions, lectures, deadlines, and other pressures. Treat the remedial program as a game in which the subject, other household members, and yourself are the players. Utilize laughter to keep failed efforts from short-circuiting the course. Laugh at your own foibles and elicit such responses from the other participants. Everyone in this game is a winner. As you proceed, you may discover a very pleasant fact: learning is fun. Get started. Your child has nothing to lose but the constraints that bind him.

11

Home
The Effective Learning Center

A Problem Exists

Mrs. Bennett's voice betrayed her exasperation at learning that her son performed inadequately at school.

"I asked Miss Leady why Josh isn't doing better. Do you know what she said?"

"I wasn't there," responds her husband.

"Of course you weren't there. That's just a figure of speech. Maybe if you'd listen . . ." Her eyes command her mouth to close. Josh, who had been sitting nearby waiting to hear the discussion, is now leaving the room. Both wife and husband grasp the possible significance of this everyday occurrence. As their heads follow their departing offspring, they make visual contact. The unspoken message is mutual and clear. Maybe we're doing something wrong. Let's resume this later—in private.

With Josh and his little sister put to bed, the Bennetts resume their conversation about Josh.

"What else did she say?" queries the now serious father.

"Well, she said his test scores were very low. He doesn't concentrate, and he's not motivated."

"But there's nothing wrong with him?" Mr. Bennett asks, seeking confirmation of something he wants to be true.

"That's what she said. No learning disability. No known handicaps. Just an underachiever."

"And he's way up there in brain power? Right?"

"Well, she didn't say it that way. She said his IQ is above average."

"But he can do better work. Above average, right?"

"I suppose so; if he's motivated, that is."

"How do we get him to be motivated?"

"I don't know."

The father ponders the meager information available for a few moments. "Somebody is doing something wrong."

Before he can suggest a possible culprit, Mrs. Bennett blurts out, "Maybe we are."

Guilt

"I guess if your child is an underachiever, you are an underachieving parent," laments the disconsolate mother. The woman across my desk has a master's degree in marketing, a middle-management position in a manufacturing company, and a freshly issued divorce decree.

"I had her in a private school but she didn't seem to like it. Lorna is now back in public school but not doing any better. The only person I can hold accountable is myself."

Another parent expresses her frustration with jab-like statements. "I went to the school. I talked to the teacher. I talked to the counselor. I sent him to a tutoring center. I've talked to him. I didn't make any headway. Nothing I do helps."

"I really didn't need this problem with Dave," says a third parent. "I just don't know what to do. I've got so many things to worry about, I don't know which has priority."

According to street-wisdom advice, if something is amiss, find a scapegoat. Numerous candidates are available to blame for poor education:

- Teachers
- Teacher unions and federations

- Politicians
- Rich people
- Poor people
- Taxpayers
- Tax evaders
- College professors
- Textbook publishers
- Yourself

A workable argument can be constructed to point an accusing finger at any group on the list or, if you prefer, justification is available to spread the culpability. Certainly, as a parent, you have some of the responsibility. But what has the educational system been doing? The world is changing rapidly. All politicians at all levels favor improving our schools. Almost everyone agrees that the school system as a whole is failing to meet current needs. As an individual, or a couple, you can't turn the system around, but you can help *your* child.

Ineffectual Advice

"I gave Josh everything they said he should have," says Mrs. Bennett, wondering why her efforts are fruitless.

"He has a quiet part of the house to work in, his own desk, good light, and all the materials and reference books he needs. I bought him bookcases, storage cabinets, and a tape recorder."

The distraught parent has created a complete study center for her son but no improvement has resulted. She hasn't done anything wrong. What she hasn't done accounts for the lack of academic achievement on the part of her child. She has merely solved the wrong problems.

There are, in fact, some children who find working at home extremely trying because of noise, disruptions, and the general lack of favorable conditions. These children may be helped by such improvements. Josh had no such problem. He came from an upper middle class family. Ample work space and a generally favorable climate for homework already existed. Josh's parents found that just improving the surroundings did not produce better grades. Making good conditions better is scratching a nonexistent itch. The focus has to be on a child's particular weakness.

Physical conditions for homework should be reasonable. Certainly, the learner needs light, a place to sit comfortably and a flat surface to spread out his materials. Desks are helpful but not vital. For many scholars, kitchen tables have held the source of food for thought as well as for the stomach. Provide the best conditions for your circumstances; they need not be ideal.

Parents are subjected to unsolicited advice from many sources. Some of the suggestions are simplistic, such as "He's just lazy. Make him work." Some are useless. "Accept the fact that he's just an underachiever." Some have a service to sell. "Send him to our learning center." Other offerings have value but not in isolation. "Build his self-esteem."

An underachiever is not likely to respond to amorphous efforts to help him. There is no equivalent of an antibiotic to kill the source of the problem. The child needs a program that is both comprehensive and easy to administer.

Preliminary Steps

First, forget the blame. Though a number of people may have contributed to the problem, blaming them will not help the situation.

Second, unburden yourself from a feeling of helplessness. There's much you can do which, as you make progress, will defuse the frustration.

Third, decide that you will follow a blueprint based on the remedial technique offered. Adapt the scheme to fit your own personality and that of your child.

Fourth, anticipate the double dividend. You will gain the satisfaction of watching your child improve and the bonus of being drawn closer to him.

Fifth, establish your home as a learning base for your child. The people in your home, and their interaction with the child in question, will play a major role in the success of your endeavor. Set aside all the bits of nebulous advice you've received and focus your efforts on a cohesive plan.

Set the Stage

Reflect on the mood, character, and atmosphere of your home from your child's standpoint, especially with regard to his relationship with you. The ambience of his environment plays a crucial part in the educational reversal. Start with general improvements as indicated:

1. Make the necessary changes in the learning center—your home. Here is one place where your child will polish his individual style. He will develop an ability to organize the multiplicity of stimuli he receives everyday. He will form lifelong habits and master skills in listening, computation, expressing his ideas, reading, and thinking.

2. Reinforce a sense of security in your child by helping him to see himself as a valued member of the family. He should reach this conclusion himself by sensing the attitudes of the people around him.

3. Work toward developing a cooperative spirit and optimism in the household but don't pretend that all is well when the child knows it isn't. Acknowledge that an unsatisfactory condition exists but don't exaggerate its importance. Consider the child's inadequate work level as merely a temporary annoyance.

4. Avoid embarrassing your child. Counseling should be handled in private. Don't let too much time elapse between a misdeed and the correction. For example, "You didn't tell me the teacher gave you a note for me. We'll discuss this the moment we get home."

5. Play the role of a parent guiding her child. Your child's pals should be his contemporaries and you're obviously too old for the job.

6. Set rules and guidelines about play time and study time that your child can understand and be prepared to enforce them. Be very understanding, very helpful, and very firm.

7. Anticipate challenges to your regulations such as, "But Billy's mother lets him do it." Don't get trapped into arguing whether Bill's mother lets him do it or not. She is probably arguing with her child about what you are allowing your youngster to do.

8. Make your child understand that you have expectations about his school performance. These expectations should be reasonable, based on a careful assessment of his capabilities.

9. Adjust the expectations you have for your child with time. If you find a specific talent, nurture it. For instance, your son may never be a concert pianist but he may still find enjoyment in playing the piano. Much of what he learns will be for his own pleasure rather than for a career.

10. Emphasize, whenever possible, efficient ways he may reach his goals. Whenever something new arises, discuss the strategy he might employ.

11. Help your child create desirable learning habits, such as attacking a task promptly, searching for his own errors and requesting help only after he's tried everything himself. Praise all of his efforts at self-reliance and offer other rewards too, such as specific items and privileges.

12. Promise only those rewards you can deliver. By not fulfilling rightful expectations you could lower your child's motivational level.

13. Show that you, too, are a person. You, too, have moods, dislikes, and disappointments. He will come to understand that everyone has feelings similar to his own. Share only those feelings and thoughts of your own that are appropriate for a child of his age. A disagreement with a spouse is not the concern of a seven-year-old.

14. Avoid using your child to satisfy your own needs. Having him perform for others when he is unready or untalented is a reflection of your own conceit. Polish your ego some other way.

15. Avoid rambling when you converse with your child. Remember he has a limited attention span.

16. Avoid showing frustration related to his work. Offer constructive suggestions. Note weaknesses in his thinking but phrase your comments as an advisor, not as a judge.

17. Avoid overprotection. Your child must be exposed to reasonable hurdles and should learn to make his own educational decisions. However, you should not abdicate your responsibility as a parent. Sometimes you will have to employ a veto.

18. Avoid locking yourself into one theory or approach to

learning. There are no absolute and totally correct instructional procedures applicable to all children.

Wrap-Up

Searching for those responsible for your child's lack of achievement may yield no dividends. Instead, start turning your home into a learning center.

Your home should not be a replication of a classroom. You may purchase various reference materials and technological instruments if you wish, but these are not vital.

Parental guidance is essential to the learning process. You must steer the youngster to keep him on course. He will then learn to make decisions as he confronts everyday challenges.

The most important contribution you can offer is to involve yourself in the learning process. Lessons can be planned from everything that happens in the home.

Parents are the child's chief guides for the journey along the path of development. This guiding function diminishes as the child grows and develops self-sufficiency. The systems he learns as a child will be utilized long after your fledgling has left the nest.

12

Developing an Interest in Learning

The Scenic Route

In a classic experiment, behavioral scientists placed hungry rats into a maze containing food in a far corner. Drawn by the aroma of the food, the rats scurried about the various passageways searching, almost frantically, for an opening to the waiting meal. Using trial and error, they found a route to their target.

The laboratory animals, again hungry, were returned to the maze another day. Demonstrating their recall powers, the rats, without hesitation, sped along the previously discovered path to their dinner. The experimenters learned something valuable about these creatures and their memories, but there was more to come.

When these experienced rodents were given tidbits to eat before entering the maze, they surprised their observers by changing the route to the food. Their appetites somewhat assuaged by the morsels, they chose to explore the maze by following avenues not yet traversed. The creatures still wanted the fare at the end but were in no hurry. They wanted to know what else was in the maze. The rats were curious!

If an animal can become curious, wouldn't a human be even

more so? Jean Piaget, who studied our own species, viewed the mind as always working. It does not wait to be activated. Just as the heart pumps and glands secrete without conscious instruction, so too does the mind think. The mind never stops querying and investigating. Recent studies reveal that this superlative natural computer is functioning at full speed even when a person sleeps. People are not machines waiting for the switch to turn on the current. They are alive and active, not static. Human inquisitiveness is a prime force in learning. The renowned psychologist, Abraham Maslow, made the observation that curiosity is a powerful motivator and does not have to be taught: ''The needs to know and to understand are seen in late infancy and childhood, perhaps even more strongly than in adulthood.''

You, as a parent, need not teach curiosity. The physical mechanism—that ever-questioning brain—is already there. You do not have to encourage curiosity. *You need only provide opportunities for your child to observe, explore, examine, manipulate, and experiment.* Sometimes you will have to be directly involved to make these opportunities possible. The time spent with your child will not only be satisfactory but will provide a learning experience for both of you and will help create a special bond that can last a lifetime.

Those Natural Drives

Curiosity is one of the proven built-in motivators. Many psychologists believe people are also motivated by internal drives that demand satisfaction. These forces energize the individual who seeks to satisfy them. A typical drive is hunger. Sigmund Freud pointed to sexual drives as a primary force that moves individuals.

Some researchers embrace the view that humans are also motivated by *external* stimuli associated with basic needs. Competition is a typical external stimulus. Success in competition induces the individual to repeat the effort.

You need not be a research psychologist to understand motivation. For example, you know when certain aromas trigger hunger in your child. As an interested parent, you want to discover the ''aromas'' of learning. You want your child to learn skills and absorb knowledge that he will be able to transfer to other settings.

Take the case of a toddler encountering a toy chest with a lid closed by a latch. To open the box, he must swing the latch away from a retaining pin. It is not his desire to decipher the latch and the pin mechanism. His only interest lies in retrieving his toys from the chest. But in order to satisfy his curiosity, he must first solve the latch puzzle, whether he realizes it or not. Once this skill is learned he will always know how to open his toy chest. He will then also know how to open the kitchen cabinets, since they employ a similar latch. All the child must do is apply the same principle he used to open the toy chest. Little does he know he's opened much more than just a toy chest. He's opened up a whole new realm of learning.

Once the child has found a solution, he experiences the exultation of success. This triumph leads to a new reinforcement of his interest and a new found confidence in his abilities. The child now adds this technique to his storehouse of solutions that he'll utilize in the future. That addition motivates the learner to try and solve another problem.

As the latch-opening toddler grows, his curiosity grows commensurate with his age and improved abilities. He applies old experiences in combination to resolve more sophisticated challenges. Curiosity cannot be taught, but it is inherent and serves as a base for the entire learning process.

If your child is innately curious, has internal drives, and is moved by external stimuli, why isn't he motivated to succeed in school at a level corresponding to his ability? He has either missed something vital while constructing his ladder of learning, is too bright for his school placement, thinks differently than most children, has an underlying problem, and/or has had some unfortunate learning experiences. Your task as a parent is to counter and mitigate whatever element, known or unknown, that has circumscribed your child's innate academically related inquisitiveness.

Some reminders: Review the child's present environmental exposure and start making changes and additions. His environment is the aggregate of his surroundings and everything he comes in contact with that may influence him. Ask questions and examine the answers as fairly as you can. Do the people and conditions surrounding your child encourage his natural curiosity?

Consider that:

- A child comes equipped with the urge to comprehend his environment and everything in it.
- This urge is a natural force requiring no particular parental instruction.
- A hungry young mind will devour all the new skills and information it can grasp.
- Learning is similar to the little snowball rolling down a hill, attracting more snow and growing larger as it rolls. Learning expands as more is added to the core.
- Each bit of insight gained by a child brings instant gratification which reinforces the desire for more.
- The child, usually subconsciously, comes to understand that learning frequently produces intrinsic rewards by indulging the ego, broadening the thought processes, and gratifying yearnings.
- Learning frequently produces material rewards.

Motivation Is Fundamental to Learning

1. Motivation is the natural consequence of interest which is awakened by discovery. Children need opportunities to discover.

2. Motivation is intricately involved with learning. Motivation can be negative, such as "do this or else." Positive motivation is not only more desirable but is usually more effective.

3. Children are apt to be motivated when they detect the possibility of satisfaction or rewards. Goals must be attainable. Extrinsic rewards include material items and special privileges.

4. Intrinsic rewards are also a major motivator. These include the excitement of discovery, the satisfaction of curiosity, the feeling of accomplishment, anticipation of feeling any of the above.

5. Needs propel motivation. Some needs are the result of internal drives. Curiosity is a cognitive need that demands

satisfaction. The child wants organization and explanations. He wants to fit into the world he perceives.

6. Parents can motivate their youngsters by setting examples. Many parents bring work home with them. Some have an office in the home. The mind of the child sees this as grownup homework. One youngster, having watched her father practicing speech deliveries in front of a mirror, adopted the method for herself. No one told her to prepare for an oral presentation the night before by talking to the mirror. She merely followed her model.

7. Success is a motivator. If a child resolves issues using his own resources, in his own style, and is free to design and experiment with solutions, he may be more motivated than if he'd received tangible rewards. The child starts life in a passive world where everything is done for him. Gradually, he exercises freedom and makes choices. The process stimulates him to continue. The drive to achieve is self-perpetuating.

8. In order for motivation to be sustained it must continue to be challenging and goal-oriented. If the learner finds a task too easy and the goal is not redirected, the motivation tends to become extinguished.

9. Praise acts as a motivator. The young child wants to please his parents and teachers but, if the praise is overdone, it may lose its impact.

10. A child is concerned mostly with the present. To have meaning, the motivation must be associated with the "now." Carrots in the future are not much of a motivator.

Parental Actions to Promote Motivation

Ask yourself some questions and provide honest and realistic answers:

- Is your child allowed to listen to the experiences of others (age-appropriate, of course) in the household? Is he permitted to pose his own queries and does he receive suitable replies?
- Does he have siblings, cousins, and friends with whom he can share experiences? Does he have opportunities to meet with and talk with these children?

- Is he encouraged to pursue hobbies and read about people, animals, and events that interest him? Are provisions made for him to discuss his interests?
- Are there neighborhood activities available that he would like to be part of? Is participation in these events fostered by the climate in his home?
- Does he spend more time in front of the television set than you think suitable? Are alternative activities readily available to him?
- Are desirable reading materials available that he might choose on impulse?
- Are there family activities that might attract his attention and spark his interests?

You can fill in the gaps you find by your own analysis and then expand his environment. Television may not be the ogre complainers contend. But, the tube lacks the stimulation of actually being there. The sense of participating, the sharing, the anticipation are only experienced at an actual event or site. Children can learn well from words, pictures, and sounds but a reinforcing emotional element is added when they themselves are present. When you can, take them there.

Take them where? Take them everywhere you think is proper. Don't overlook all the exciting possibilities in your own familiar neighborhood. Visitors from distant places may travel to your area to see what you ignore, "because it was always there." More than half the population of the Delaware River Valley has never seen the Liberty Bell located in easily reachable center-city Philadelphia. Relatively few residents of eastern Pennsylvania, northern New Jersey, and southeast New York have actually been to the Statue of Liberty. Many of these same people will travel thousands of miles to see the California redwoods or visit the Grand Canyon. Though travel experiences are valuable, you should not overlook local areas of interest. Take your children where? Everywhere.

Accompany him or arrange for him to be taken to neighborhood and reasonably close attractions. A mall and other shopping centers can serve as a magnet to capture his attention. Many of these establishments plan special attractions for children on nonschool days. Their public relations office will happily supply you with brochures and data on events being planned. These happenings include children's concerts, celebrity appearances, usually from a local television station, clowns and comics, and special theme presentations. Your child may not be interested in an antique exhibit but may be excited by a show on the latest toys.

Be a tourist in your own home grounds. Historical sites, usually overlooked by long-time residents of a community, may appeal to youngsters. Almost every area has something: a Civil War or Revolutionary War battlefield, statues commemorating some significant event, or the first sawmill in the state. Information prepared for visitors is available at your nearest chamber of commerce. Check the tours in your own or nearby city. Ask your travel agent for help. The possibilities will surprise those who have never considered them.

Visit the commonplace. Are there botanical gardens, aquariums, and zoos nearby? You certainly have police and fire stations and perhaps a military base. Tours are sometimes arranged by utility companies and industry. Visitors are usually welcomed at specified times. Call first and ask for a public relations officer. The advice they offer will be extremely helpful. And don't forget your local libraries and museums.

Take special note of sporting events. There are exciting competitions in every season of the year and you need not have a professional team in your area. Try attending high school and college games for an inexpensive and stimulating outing. Baseball may be the national pastime and football and basketball have a huge following, but there are other worthwhile sports, such as tennis, ice hockey, swimming competitions, and bowling. Many elementary-level children visiting a massive stadium for the first time are stimulated by the size, appearance, vivid color, and peripheral vision that is not apparent on the electronic box. New and exciting doors may swing open.

Take your child to a movie theater. Going to the movies at one time was an American ritual for young children, especially on Saturday afternoons. This has been replaced, in large measure, by television and movies played on VCRs, but the theater still has its place. Mixing with people, crunching popcorn, and watching the big screen is enlightening and entertaining. For some children, especially at the younger end of the scale, this is a new and wondrous experience. "Look, Mom, they're playing a tape on that giant tube!"

Try taking him to live theater which he may find quite intriguing. Children are familiar with elementary school plays, but an experience with competent acting and direction is unlike any other. There is, arguably, only one Broadway, but if that is out of your reach geographically and financially, there are road performances by professionals in many cities and some quite good neighborhood players. A visit to a suitable performance may provide new horizons for your child. Don't overlook live music festivals and country fairs for entertainment and new experiences.

Take your child to sites considered mundane by some adults but actually interesting and eye opening for a youngster. These places include train stations, airports, cab stands, and truck depots. The little ones are attracted to everyday routines such as baggage handling, radio communications, loading platforms, and fueling.

Plan vacations and weekend jaunts to include visits to areas unfamiliar to your child. Picnicking and playing on beaches is commonplace to many children, but not all. If appropriate, plan for such excursions. If circumstances prohibit these trips, there is always hiking, camping, and country drives.

Have your child join organizations for youngsters his age. You can easily find suitable neighborhood clubs, church youth groups, scouts, athletic leagues, or music and art classes.

The Chips May Differ from the Block

You cannot force an interest on a child. You can only present opportunities. Sometimes you may be surprised by the outcome.

Keith's father arranged frequent excursions for his family to places of interest. Deprived of his own hardworking father's company most of the time as a youth, he was determined to play a large role in raising his own children.

All of the family members enjoyed trips to the zoo, and one year Keith's father purchased season passes. Keith's dad had always liked the monkey island and assumed his seven-year-old son felt the same way. Like father, like—well, it was obvious. Keith thought the simian antics amusing but a deeper interest directed him elsewhere. The boy insisted on visiting the reptile house and spent several hours with his nose flattened against the viewing glass. His mother and sisters hied off to other sections while his father, fidgeting, remained with Keith. At last, the boy inadvertently provided an opportunity for the father to leave.

"How can snakes move without legs?" queried the youngster.

"Good question," the man replied. "Let's find someone to ask."

Having found an excuse to exit, the adult hustled his son toward the door.

That evening, Keith's father reflected on how a seemingly trivial incident had taught him a valuable lesson. The degree of interest and curiosity in any subject varies with individuals. He regretted terminating the visit to the snake house earlier in the day based on his own desires, not his son's.

If your child is developing an interest in an acceptable area, even though it might not be your choice, encourage him. The more interesting a topic is to an individual, the easier it is to learn. The learning procedures become transferable to other subjects and make other less interesting matters somewhat easier to master.

What Is He Asking?

Curiosity cannot be motivated with precision. Jimmy's father brought home a 15-inch globe on a stand. While the parent was certain nine-year-old Jimmy used globes in school, he thought that some additional benefits could be derived from having one in the house. A flat map, the adult knew, could not portray accurately both the size and shape of a large land mass at the same time. The globe could and would help his son develop a better understanding of astronomy as well.

The father was pleased one day when he found Jimmy spinning the globe, stopping the rotation and examining the sphere carefully. The lad's expression was one of curiosity. Pointing to the replica of the earth, he asked, "Dad, what's inside of it?"

The father considered momentarily before replying. He wanted to give a factual but understandable answer.

"Well, under the earth's crust are layers of hard rock. Then, deeper, maybe four or five miles down is molten rock called magma and then . . ."

"No, Dad. I don't mean the real earth. I mean this globe right here. How do they make it? What's inside of it?"

Listen carefully to your child's question and respond to what the youngster really wants to know. A hoary educational joke relates how eight-year-old Sara approached her mother one day asking, "Mom, where did I come from?" The parent was perturbed but quickly gained her composure. A child's sex questions, she had read, should be answered concisely but accurately. She then proceeded with a modern version of the birds and the bees. Sara listened patiently and, when her mother was finished, responded, "But you didn't tell me what I want to know. Megan said she came from Boston. Didn't we live someplace before?"

Intensifying Interest

Always provide an opportunity for your child to tell you about his journey. If he's bubbling over and unable to describe anything coherently at the moment, let him go on. Don't dampen his enthusiasm. Later, when the excitement has subsided, have him repeat the information he might have related earlier instead of a volley of confused words.

Ask clarifying questions. Have him think about and describe segments of his experience. "Great" is not enough of a description. Get into more detail. Draw him out but don't take over the conversation. You are the listener. Be sure you understand his account. He'll be disappointed if you don't remember what he has told you.

Have him make comparisons with other trips, or people, or just feelings.

"Did you really like that?"

"Would you like to go again sometime?"

"What color was it?"

"You said 'big.' How big? Big as our house?"

"Exactly what did she say? See how close you can come to her words. Can you imitate her?"

"Was it that delicious? What did they call it? Maybe I can find the recipe in my cookbook and make it for you."

"Did you really like that? I'm sure the library has some books on it. Want to go look?"

"I'm having a difficult time picturing it. Want to draw it for me?"

"I'll tell you what. Why don't you speak into the tape recorder. Then we'll both listen to it again."

"That was interesting. I did the very same thing when I was about your age. We'll have to discuss this again and compare notes."

If your child returns home unenthusiastic, try to find out why. The attraction may not be his thing. There are others. You're looking for areas he finds interesting which in turn will create zest for learning. The process of how to learn is transferable. Your goal is to open some doors, but you can't open them all. Some avenues will lead nowhere but sometimes he will find stimulation by taking the scenic route.

Wrap-Up

Children are naturally curious. This inborn desire to inquire, search, and scrutinize motivates them into action.

Your offspring may differ from you in interests. Your task is to expand his environment in a general way. Allow him the freedom to make specific choices from acceptable activities.

Internal and external excitation are always at work and affecting your child. You have some, but limited control over these drives.

Your child may have missed a vital rung in the ladder of learning, had some unfortunate experiences, or been misplaced in his academic setting. Your challenge is to adjust his learning patterns by providing motivation-type activities.

- Review your child's surroundings as objectively as you can, from his perspective, and make the adjustments and changes that are possible.
- Satisfy your child's questions by responding directly to his query; resist adding on items you consider "good to know."

- Avoid asking your child, "Why do you want to know that?" If it's proper for him to know, tell him. If an answer would be inappropriate for his age, tell him that.
- Provide opportunities for the child to discover new aspects of the world. When he becomes excited by a newfound interest it will then serve as the motivating factor for him to learn about it. The process of learning is never in a void. Although your child may focus on one element, there are always spillovers into concomitant learning. He may want to know about trucks, but he's bound to learn words that are employable elsewhere.

13

Sails, Not Anchors

Laying Down the Law

"John! You're grounded. You're going to stay in the whole week and that includes the weekend. You're going to study, study, study. I've had enough of this fooling around. I've tried the modern stuff. No more choices. You'll do it my way! Understand? You'll come home directly from school; you'll do whatever your mother wants done in the house, and then you'll get to your schoolwork. You'll only stop for dinner and then you'll get back to homework. Until bedtime. That's it. End of discussion."

The ten-year-old's father felt the satisfying release of his internal pressure as he concluded his torrent of regulations. Perhaps, he thought, he ought to instill the fear of punishment to come. No. It was time to apply the brakes. Better not overdo it, he cautioned himself. The brakes failed. Despite his self-warning, he added, "And, young man, you're not too big for a good old-fashioned spanking. And I mean it!" He did. Pleased with himself, he turned to the audience, his wife. "See? That's done. Now we'll get somewhere."

The child's mother silently questioned the effectiveness of the lecture and threats. These tactics had never helped before.

But something had to work. John wasn't taking school seriously, as reflected by his grades.

The boy stifled his yawn. This will blow away soon, he mused. He was feeling his empty stomach's plea for satisfaction. What's for dinner? he wondered. He knew better than to ask the question at this moment.

Some children accept their scholastic shortcomings without noticeable effect. They've learned not to care. Typically, they announce, "I have better things to do." Many of these children respond to out-of-school activities and, on the surface, appear to be happy. Submerged, well beneath the veneer, may be feelings of skepticism about their academic ability. They adjust by downplaying the importance of school and concentrating on events elsewhere.

John, for instance, was socially active. He was outgoing and gregarious with a broad range of interests. John was eager for new activities and willing to accept challenges without undue hesitation. He enjoyed sports, games, trips, movies, camping, and fishing. Because of his promptness and enthusiasm he was frequently described as "Johnny-on-the-spot." John did well in most ventures. At school, he just managed to get by.

John's father, using a tried but untrue method, felt that his hand was a potential motivator. Negative motivation does indeed work in some situations. Pain-avoidance is understood by rats on an electric grill and by prisoners who have experienced solitary confinement. Your child is neither a rat nor a prisoner.

The concern here is only with punishment related to learning and not misbehavior. In general, punishment should not be associated with schoolwork. Misapplied, punishment could counter many remedial efforts. Learning should satisfy curiosity, be fun, and be rewarding, not something extraneous to the life of the child. He should not engage in studying only under duress.

Punishment can get out of hand and sometimes does. The tendency is to increase the "sentence" when favorable results are not forthcoming, thereby magnifying the problem and rendering the threat useless.

"If you don't get to work immediately, you'll have to stay in twice as long."

Had John's father carried out his warnings, the boy would have been grounded until he was 30.

The child who consistently underachieves, not surprisingly, is likely to have developed a strong negative attitude toward school. His experiences with unsatisfactory academic work have imbued him with the feeling that education is not his strong point. He must look elsewhere for success. Children such as John become immune to haranguing and threats. They adjust to doing poorly and become accustomed to being berated. They may find gratification in other activities. School is something to be endured until they are old enough to escape its grasp.

A Sail

If the natural urge to satisfy curiosity needs assistance, you may employ a reward system. The positive benefits of punishment without the injury may be obtained by setting up a schedule of earned credits.

Instead of penalizing poor work, reward satisfactory productivity. Aware points or credits for homework completed. Award additional points for clarity, good handwriting, neatness, and extra work done by the child. The youngster accumulates these points for a period of time, perhaps a week or two. He then exchanges his credits for a prize—something he wants. It may be a toy, a trip, or a chance to watch a television program "past his normal bedtime" on the weekend. The possible rewards are inexhaustible. Be sure he knows what they are, make sure he wants them, and doesn't get them for any reason other than success in doing homework. Keep the process simple.

"I know you want to go to the party on Saturday but you haven't earned enough credits."

"How many do I need?"

"Let's look at the sheet. Parties require one hundred."

"How many do I have?"

"Sixty. If you do your homework in full throughout the week, you'll earn thirty more credits."

"That's close enough, isn't it. Ninety?"

"No. The sheet says one hundred."

"I'll borrow ten against next week's work. Okay?"

"Sorry. This bank doesn't make loans."

"Isn't there anything I can do?"

"Let's see. If you work on your science project Saturday morning and really get something done, you can earn ten, maybe even twenty credits. It's a good idea to build up a reserve for future use."

In education, using work credits to earn a prize is known as a token economy. In psychology, it is viewed as a variant of operant conditioning. In your home, it's called good sense. For me, it's using what works.

Academies have a history of using demerits, but this is strictly punishment and should be avoided. "You get ten demerits" sounds too much like "You'll be given ten lashes." Stay with the positive. Good work brings adults good pay, or is supposed to. Overtime brings in additional compensation. Maybe. Let the child earn his remuneration in the way of desirable rewards. A fair system will be effective if the parent doesn't allow exceptions and stays with it long enough for the child to internalize its meaning.

Simple Solutions

Greg's parents, unhappy about their child's substandard progress, seek help. They visit the school and meet with the nine-year-old's teacher.

PARENTS: We're very disappointed in Greg's class work. Is there anything you can tell us? Is there something you didn't write on his report card?

TEACHER: No, not really. Greg is certainly capable of better work.

PARENTS: Then what's the problem?

TEACHER: Greg is one of those children who just doesn't do his best. These children are quite common, you know. He is far from being alone.

PARENTS: Why?

TEACHER: Children go through stages. Right now, Greg's

interest is not in school. Does he get excited by outside
activities?

PARENTS: Not really. He spends much of his time in his
room. He seems withdrawn.

TEACHER: Oh. Perhaps that, too, is just a stage. Look, why
don't I arrange a meeting with the school counselor.
Perhaps she can help.

Greg's parents meet with the counselor ten days later. They
find her prepared and pleasant. She has already examined their
child's records and has met twice with Greg. After reviewing
the child's school history, the counselor offers an analysis.
Greg, in her opinion, is a perfectly normal child. She can find
nothing seriously wrong with him. "Not everyone," she
explains, "is a 'student.' Some children are very bright but not
the scholarly type." Encourage him but be patient, is the
summation of her advice.

Seeing that the parents are not satisfied, the counselor notes
that she could arrange for a psychological examination to be
administered by the school district but the waiting list is long.
If the parents wish, they can see a private psychologist but
would have to pay a fee. Greg's parents opt for a private
analysis.

A psychometrician administered a battery of tests covering
intellectual levels, emotional stability, personality, and interests. A psychotherapist talked to Greg at length and, after
carefully examining the test results, offers her conclusion.

Greg is not in need of treatment. He is emotionally stable. He
does, perhaps, engage in too much day-dreaming, but the child
has a clear understanding of the difference between fantasy and
reality. The tests reveal no dysfunction that would explain his
curtailed learning.

Greg has superior intelligence. Since he is not learning-
disabled, emotionally disturbed, or the product of a severely
disadvantaged environment, he is merely an underachiever.
Both the teacher and the counselor, explains the psychologist,
have been accurate in their judgments.

"What do we do to help him?" queried the parents.

As millions have heard, the remedial suggestions centered
around encouragement, patience, and a suitable study place at
home. "And," adds the psychologist, "give him lots of love."

Unlike John, who played the role of school hater but fared well in nonacademic activities, Greg felt sorry for himself. He began to sulk and gradually lost interest in the pursuits of his friends. Greg withdrew and spent many hours alone with his fantasies. He became a hero in a make-believe world. He was a star pitcher, a boxing champion, and, according to the sports journalists, the finest quarterback of the century. Although all people from time to time engage in fantasies, Greg went a little further. While he approached the border of mental illness, he never crossed it. But his dream world did occupy too much of the time he needed for socializing and learning.

A parent of a "Greg" type child needs more than a standby prescription such as "Provide lots of love." Love is medicinal only if it has been absent and its lack is a cause of the problem. Make it clear to your child that he is loved but don't force stale expressions of love at irrelevant times. Words without emotional backup wear thin quickly and can be counterproductive. Children see through routine, counterfeit, or perfunctory expressions. True feelings are revealed in your eyes, attitude, and such gestures as impromptu hugs.

The Stings

An effective course of action includes reducing the number and ameliorating the importance of negatives directed at your child in his home. Success for anyone depends largely on one's view of himself. Your child is no different. He requires a reasonable level of self-esteem to approach a task with confidence. Your aim is to help him reach this level.

Reexamine the parent-child relationship. Display an interest in your child's activities. Question him about them and hold discussions. The younger the child the more he'll be willing to share with you. Refrain from demanding to know everything. He's entitled to privacy and secrets. Judge his feelings of security, stability, and freedom from undue anxiety by your observations.

Enlist the cooperation of everyone in the household to erase all vestiges of these negatives. This goal may never be fully attained but substantial improvements are likely to occur with reasonable effort. You should avoid, if possible, singling out the one child. Instead of "Let's not pick on Rick anymore," urge the family group not to pick on each other. You may not gain complete cooperation from Rick's siblings but you can censor your own opinions. Make a sincere effort to curb derogatory comments and displays of dissatisfaction.

Barbs can come in many forms, such as through remarks, gestures, or expectations. It is easy to puncture a child's balloon of self-value. Some children can take the hurt and some can't.

Don't belittle your child. Put-downs may confirm the child's suspicion that he really can't do the work expected of him. One-liners, without intention, may strike at your child's emotional substructure.

"Sorry, Rick. I better have Zack (his younger brother) do this."

"I guess you take after your Uncle Harry. He could never do anything right either."

"Look, Rick. Try to think. This number has to be carried over. See?"

"All right. I suppose you did as well as you can."

"Ask the clerk for nail polish remover—wait a minute. I better write it down."

Expunge the negative "corrections." Assaults on the ego of a child are commonplace by parents who lost patience with a child's performance. Damage to the psyche may never heal. Put a full-time censoring device on your mouth.

More Sails

Many scholars hold that the theories of the late Jean Piaget are to learning and development as the theories of Albert Einstein are to astrophysics. Piaget opened many doors to understanding mental growth but one of his most salient observations has been underutilized in schools. The Swiss biopsychologist stressed that the emotional aspects of learning are inextricably connected with the thinking process. To succeed in a formal class setting, the emotional components of learning must be on a par with the student's thought processes.

You can do more in this vital area of emotional support than schools or tutoring centers. If you can bring significant improvement to only one area, this is it. The techniques of efficient learning attack skills are discussed in the chapter on homework, but everything you attempt will have only limited success unless you consider the emotional side of learning. A child is by nature curious, but he must be curious about something. He must be motivated to satisfy his curiosity and reap the internal and material rewards of success. If he is convinced that he is incapable of hitting the target, he probably won't, even if he possesses the innate skill required. Lack of confidence impedes practically all learning and this state exists because the child possesses a poor self-portrait. His level of self-esteem must be raised. This essential factor integral to learning is the mainsail that will carry him forward.

Self-Esteem

Underachievers, as individuals, refuse to fit into neatly designed molds. Individualized programs are necessary for individual children. The overall remedial strategies may be similar but the tactics must fit the specific situation. A child who underperforms in school probably lacks some aspect of self-esteem. As a parent, you may already have significant clues to explain the behavior of your child.

You know if your youngster is aggressive or shy, energetic or torpid, punctual or tardy, dependable or unreliable. He may feel, without necessarily expressing it openly, that schoolwork causes him problems and that he has no way to circumvent these obstacles. He may be socially and athletically successful but may also realize that he lacks some element that would enable him to perform well in school.

This inner feeling of academic inadequacy may be camouflaged by boisterous behavior, bragging, and exaggerated disinterest in class work. Some children, to cover up these submerged feelings, resort to misbehavior, belligerency, or clowning. Professional comedians sometimes acknowledge that they started by resorting to jokes and pranks because they couldn't adjust to school.

"I can't do that," is another commonly expressed feeling of these children. Their tendency is to avoid challenges or surrender to the first obstacle. You, the parent, must reverse this mental state by building confidence.

Find something in your child's area of interest to develop. Encourage him to do what he wants to do provided it's an activity that meets with your approval. Most children will pursue an area of interest rather willingly. Try to produce confidence, to have the child feel the elation of success. Spread ointment on a bruised ego.

A Taste of Winning

If your child has withdrawn, has few or no friends, or avoids competition, he must be subjected to planned motivation. You may, for instance, promote the competitive spirit in him via selective commercial games. Toy stores display numerous activities appropriate for the various age levels. These make excellent birthday and Christmas gifts. If he wins a fair share of competitive games while playing with others, your mission is accomplished. If he loses too often and displays dissatisfaction, some overt action on your part is indicated.

Avoid letting him win, which is more than just being dishonest. He'll eventually decipher that ploy and his ego will be further impaired. Instead, do what adults do in many activities from chess to the golf course. Provide a handicap. He will require less to win or start with more advantages than his opponent. Thus, he will gain the experience of winning without the deceit. The handicap can be modified as he gains confidence.

Once a child finds he is winning at a competitive activity, the urge to continue playing may become compelling. He may want to engage in that activity endlessly to the exclusion of others. He is enjoying his new-found skill—too much. As a parent, you are still in charge. Find other games and activities that may make him a winner.

You want your child to know, also, that losing sometimes doesn't mean his efforts should terminate. He should "come back fighting" and try again. You can regulate this by changing the handicap, providing stiffer opposition, or providing a new game. The child just has to win sometime at something. He has to feel that it is possible for him to win and then savor the feeling when it does occur.

Work Attitudes

Getting started in individualized thinking-writing endeavors required by assignments sometimes is difficult. Adults are commonly confronted with this problem. For underachieving children, it's the norm. These children start playing with no hesitation and, when it's time to do homework, will volunteer immediately for any other activity.

Schoolwork has become an unpleasant, unrewarding, and frequently frustrating task. But that is only one reason. For some, the very act of being alone with their minds, of depending on their own initiative and of being evaluated solely on their own performance is alarming. They feel naked, exposed, a revealed target.

Sharing an assignment with others acts as a lubricant as it reduces the friction. The sharing removes the spotlight from the person and allows him to hide his misgivings under the cloak of numbers. The feeling is not unknown among adults. Being part of a group or audience provides anonymity and allows the individual to act in ways he would avoid if acting alone. The numbers provide a communal effort where the natural leadership of some members spur on the assembly and no one is singled out for lagging behind. For instance, during a performance, one laugh, at a propitious moment, may trigger a total audience reaction. An insecure individual can then feel free to laugh without worrying if it is appropriate.

Alone, a person has the entire burden of decision making with the concomitant responsibility. For some people this takes little effort. Others have more trouble. Many writers, for example, staring at blank paper, have stated that first gear is the hardest. Yet these people, presumably, are engaged in pursuits they have chosen. Your underachieving child has not selected the task he faces. He may be reluctant to expose himself to failure.

To overcome your child's disinclination to begin, be understanding of his misgivings and work with him to lighten the task.

- Have him estimate the scope of the work while you sit with him.
- Show him that having all of the required materials readily available will save time.
- Divide lengthy assignments into segments that do not appear forbidding.
- Stay with him or close by as he masters the techniques of getting started and then completing his work.
- Act as his learning associate initially, sharing his efforts and then gradually fade from his presence as he develops confidence. Your own attitude will serve as a model for the learner. Be optimistic, pleasant, and reveal no sign that this is a chore. Be an actress. Using Franklin's "stitch" now will save inestimable hours later.
- Advance the notion that:
  Any assignment given by the teacher is at his level.
  He definitely has the ability to do the work.
  You expect him to succeed.
  Learning becomes easier as it is pursued.
  Learning is really fun.
  Learning can be used to bring current and future rewards.
- Discuss any questions he poses. Do none of the work for him but ask questions that will lead him in the right direction. Outright suggestions are permissible when nothing else works.
- Help your child understand that errors happen but need not be fatal. The first step in correcting a mistake is to admit it. Errors must be identified to analyze problems and make corrections. Your acknowledgment of a mistake that you made and your own corrective steps will serve as a valuable experience for the student. Example is still the best teacher.
- Treat any setback as a challenge rather than a collapse of his effort. If you view a stumble as a fall, so will he. Show your acceptance of mistakes and treat them as mere aberrations. He'll follow your lead. Note any areas adequately completed and use these aspects as starting points.
- Work toward a success, no matter how limited. Nothing

will get him started faster the next time than the satisfaction he feels from a degree of achievement. Acknowledge, favorably, completed and accurate work. Turn even a partial success into a triumph.

The key to a child's overcoming inertia is to be part of his group or in "partnership" with someone, such as a parent, until he experiences enough successful attempts and feels confident enough to go solo. His negatives will diminish as his confidence rises. A new spirit will carry him beyond a reluctant start and take him into an operational mode capable of sustaining his efforts throughout an assignment. You will have reprogrammed him.

Sometimes, as your child does his work without your direct supervision, he will encounter failure. You may be surprised to learn that, in some circumstances, this is a plus. One of the strongest motivators for accomplishment, as the eminent psychologist Jerome Bruner and others have noted, is failure followed by success on a subsequent try. Considerable empirical data exist to support this view. Thus, if there has been a failure, your child must try again. Once a success has been attained, a mechanism has been established that will propel the child toward more successes.

As before, break an academic challenge into components. Edge forward slowly. Show approval for each bit of improvement. Make your expectations clear. Gradually, as if contagious, they will become his expectations. He will develop an inner voice that will, throughout life, encourage him: "Yes I can. Yes I can."

You can put wind in his sails by building his complex inner structure of self-esteem. You have started by providing the flavor of winning where needed and by redirecting his approach and attitude toward his schoolwork. The next chapter will focus on the learning attack skills vital to succeeding in school and the chapter after that will add more sail, suggesting how to utilize praise, confidence, successful experiences, and encouragement. The cognitive and emotional aspects of learning are like egg yolks and egg whites—scrambled. They can be discussed individually, but in reality, cannot be separated.

Wrap-Up

You can have a major impact on how your child adapts to his educational milieu. Start your remedial procedures with the home environment.

Reduce the number and severity of the negatives your child encounters at home. To succeed, your child requires self-esteem which, in turn, is based on a feeling of security. Denigration of your child, by anyone in the household, will hamper your efforts.

The complex human organism adjusts to its experiences in a given environmental setting. The adjustment may not be the kind a parent desires for her child. The youngster may learn to avoid work and responsibility.

Adjustments, including negative ones, are not necessarily permanent. A parent with a plan can change how her child functions.

A parental plan to reverse underachievement must include the emotional aspects of learning which, though often disregarded, are intertwined with thinking.

Stringent controls over underachievers not only have a high failure rate but frequently exacerbate an already unfortunate state of affairs. The learning process should be linked to desirable activities and should, if possible, be divorced from punishment. Short-term gains, sometimes attained via rigid controls and intensive drill and application, are stopgap measures. The underachieving child, because of his innate ability, may catch up temporarily, but later will fall back to where he was, or even lower. The causes of his poor performance, if unaddressed, will still remain.

Parental thought, guidelines, and involvement are required for the implementation of a remedial plan. The parent can, with reasonable effort, teach her child how to learn. Parental involvement should decrease as the child progresses.

Underachieving children require ego massaging to change their outlook on academics. The key to the reconstruction of their self-view is experience with success. As they build confidence in their own ability, their attitude—the emotional component of learning—will improve dramatically.

14

Homework *Is* Important

Assume, based on the diagnosis you have followed in Part I, that your child is, in fact, capable of better academic work.

Don't assume that he could improve if he only wanted to.

Assume, instead, that a vital element of his learning process is underdeveloped or impaired. As explained in Part II, this attenuated link in the learning chain may be due to illness, severe stress, or unfavorable experiences. The child may have failed to master an essential part of the developmental hierarchy necessary for learning.

Schools don't teach children *how* to learn. Schools teach "tool subjects," such as reading and arithmetic, and "content subjects," such as social studies and science. School instruction is designed for groups and focuses on *what* is to be learned, not *how*.

Don't think that you must replace the teacher in order to help your child. Let the certified teacher teach arithmetic, spelling, geography, and the rest. Your efforts in this direction may be at variance with the techniques used by the child's teacher and actually impede learning. You may help occasionally on the elementary level but your role is to foster the development of learning skills. Your job is to make it possible for the teacher to teach your child, not usurp the teacher's position.

Homework

The starting point of your efforts should be your child's homework. Home assignments are based on the grade level of the student and are directly related to school topics. I have never seen a child who produces satisfactory homework remain an underachiever.

The unprepared underachiever, diving into his home assignment, will:

- Give up easily
- Do it sketchily and leave many sections incomplete
- Call ''Mom'' every three minutes
- Learn little

With a plan in place, these negative habits can be improved. (See Chapter 13 for reward systems, such as a token economy.)

Stay with your child until he completes his home assignments most of the time on his own. Then gradually withdraw as he becomes an independent learner. Your obligation should change eventually from guidance in learning strategies to consultation for special problems. Your involvement diminishes as your child gains skills.

The following steps are effective in assisting underachievers to become proficient in homework.

1. Analysis of the Assignment

Identify the essence of the problem. What is the main theme? In general, what is to be learned? Why was the assignment given? How does the assignment fit in with the work at school?

The main theme could be that the American Revolution was inevitable or that multiplication is a shortcut to unwieldy additions, or that four known forces permeate the universe. An underachiever might never have developed the habit of identifying the purpose of particular assignments. See that he does.

Separate the essential elements from the extraneous. The learner must determine, before he becomes involved, what the important elements of the task are. The fact that Jefferson had to dip his quill into ink might be of passing interest but the

consequences of the Declaration of Independence were not
related to writing instruments. Had the ballpoint pen been
invented two centuries earlier, American history probably
would be the same.

Determine, specifically, what is to be done. What questions
are to be answered? What problems need to be solved? The
child should know before beginning his task exactly what he
has to do. He should start with a clear view as to what lies
ahead. Surprises are for stories, not homework.

The learner should be able to describe the lesson and state
his goals. Reading his role from notes or a text is only an initial
step. He should be able to explain the work his way. If he can't,
he doesn't understand it sufficiently. Go back to square one.

The child should form a mental image of the completed
homework just as a hair stylist visualizes the outcome before
even starting. Jigsaw puzzles show a complete picture on the
box for a good reason. Homework, too, should not be a
mystery. The learner must know where he is going and how he
is to get there.

He should, for instance, know that when he's finished, he'll
have three pages of outline material on the story or seven
arithmetic problems spaced neatly and clearly in a prescribed
order. He should know what his ultimate goal is, be it the
causes of the War of Independence or how to carry a digit when
multiplying.

2. Plan of Action

Once the child understands the challenge, he must collect all
of the information and materials required. Are all the necessary
elements available? Where can missing information be found?
Should everything needed be accumulated before starting? In a
one-sitting assignment, the answer is usually yes.

If the problem is complex, he should create a checklist
covering all of the important points. In so doing, he will
preclude the possibility of overlooking a necessary factor. The
checklist also channels his efforts into a preplanned sequence
and is effective as a brief outline.

If the task of the learner appears too difficult for him at this
point, determine if it lends itself to subdivision. An assignment
may, in fact, appear to be overwhelming. As a guiding parent,
you can help the child disassemble the monster so that he may

tackle manageable segments one at a time. Otherwise, faced with a seemingly impossible chore, the underachiever may quit before he has actually begun.

The youngster needs help initially in developing a strategy to attack the problem. After some practice, he will become quite efficient. The questions to be asked vary with the assignment but should include the following in language appropriate for his age:

- How were similar tasks handled in the past?
- What techniques may be useful now?
- What alternative methods may be effective?
- What is the most effective system for this work?
- Should the written material be underlined?
- Should an outline be created?
- Should supplemental data be extracted from a reference book?
- Should pertinent facts and concepts be expanded into paragraph form?

Part of the planning requires the scheduling of work. Most elementary school assignments can be completed in one evening but if more are required, it is necessary to devise an appropriate plan. Review the calendar of family activities with your child and make provision for the assigned project. Don't overallow time for each sitting, but keep some hours in reserve, perhaps during the weekend.

It is your job to help your child carry out his plan successfully. Before he begins, again, have him explain the assignment and how he will proceed. You'll find that after a few sessions, he'll be able to prepare for his work in much less time than it takes you to read these pages. But don't assume he already knows what he's supposed to do. Review it with him each session until he's sure what route to follow.

Be certain that your youngster has an understanding of the vocabulary used in the assignment. Don't ask him if he knows a word but ask if he knows the meaning. Can he use it properly? If not, send him to the dictionary or, sometimes, define it for him. Your decision should be based on the length of his assignment, the time allotted for its completion, and the frequency of the occurrence.

3. Implementing the Plan

You should help him execute his plan, but reduce your association as he gains experience.

When unexpected problems do arise, have him offer possible approaches to reach solutions. If he can't, then you should make concrete suggestions. Remember to keep your help firm but light. "Why don't you go back and recopy those numbers? Maybe you made a mistake in one of them. I've made such errors many times."

"Oops. You didn't carry the seven. See? That's a common mistake people make."

"Yes. You missed that bit of information. You keep making mistakes like that and you'll be down to my level. Don't you dare agree!"

Allow the child to follow his own system, but if he fails, suggest some different strategies. "Read the first paragraph. Now what did it say? What's important about that? Fine. Now, write one sentence to say that. Good. Now read the second paragraph."

Monitor his efforts as he completes each step. Have him explain what he is doing. If he errs, repeat the process. Openly show your confidence in him and give him an ego boost when he gets it right by himself. "Good. I knew you could do it."

Allow him to work alone as soon as he demonstrates understanding, but check on his progress from time to time. The mind has a tendency to wander and may have to be jolted back to the task at hand. Put your youngster back on the track with a joke and continually reveal your expectations of a timely, completed, and competent job. Your expectations will be fulfilled.

4. Evaluation

The rapport you establish with your child relative to schoolwork becomes crucial in evaluating his final product. The closer the two of you are, the more likely he will want to discuss his efforts and the easier it will be for you to offer constructive criticism.

• Is the job completely done?
• Did he do what he set out to do?

- Does he understand each component of the assignment?
- Does he see connections and relationships among components?
- Does he understand the underlying meaning of the assignment?
- Does he have a reasonable grasp of the important facts?
- What additional facts did he learn from the assignment?
- Where or when might this material be used again?
- Is his written work neat and clear?
- Are his grammar and spelling correct?

5. Reinforcement

Your child should be given an opportunity to tell you or someone else about his lessons. Grandparents make a great captive audience.

Look for opportune moments for him to practice what he has learned. You will be able, frequently, to relate news items and movies to lessons learned in history, civics, and geography. Arithmetic problems appear constantly in everyday life. His academic work is on a continuum and much of it depends on earlier learnings. He should be using the material he's learned repeatedly.

6. Teacher Evaluation

Homework should not be handed in at school and forgotten. Your child should get it back in a few days with his teacher's corrections and comments. Review these comments with him and have him decide how his work can be improved. Most teachers are quite pleased to have cooperative parents. Remember that teachers too, as with most of us, appreciate recognition for their extra efforts.

Wrap-Up

Homework should be taken seriously and considered an integral part of classroom work. It is a direct link to school activity and a gauge of your child's progress.

The child should start his work with an overview of the entire assignment and its objectives. He should understand the goal and purpose of his homework. Having a roadmap to learning is a fundamental principle. He should formulate a plan to complete the work in the shortest possible time, with the most understanding, and with the least parental assistance. With proper direction and practice youngsters can learn quickly.

Your efforts should be directed away from "Did you do your homework?" to:

"What did you have for homework?"
"What approach did you use?"
"Any problems?"
"Fine. Let's check it over."

The roots of learning are based on strategic skills. A systematic approach to learning is one of them. A planned system for doing homework is the beginning.

15

Hoist More Canvas

Serendipity—What I Found Out

An educational experiment I conducted was carefully planned to yield accurate results. The children being studied had emotional problems which were a probable cause of their poor school performance. The students were randomly assigned to experimental and control groups.

The experimental group was supposed to learn grammar using a software package requiring minimal teacher involvement. The control group was to be taught the same content material by traditional teacher-class interaction. All other conditions of locations, times, seating, lighting, and familiarity were equivalent. Even the teachers had been chosen because of similar personalities, experience, and competence. The study was designed to determine whether the experimental group, using the program I had developed, could learn more than the children in the classical setup during a given time frame. I was unaware of my oversight until the endeavor had been completed.

At the end of the planned period, both groups were tested with the same instrument to measure individual learning and calculate the difference between the groups. The experimental group performed as I had calculated but the control group, much to my surprise, had fared extraordinarily well. They were taught as they had always been, but had progressed far more than anticipated. Something was wrong or maybe something was right.

A review of the study revealed that the students in the typical classroom arrangement, the control group, had discovered that they were involved in a competition. Despite their emotional handicaps, they galvanized their efforts and competed as a team. They attacked their assignments with unprecedented zeal, attended to the instructor more than ever before, and worked as a unit. The spirit of cooperation blossomed. The more they succeeded, the more enthusiastic they became. Their teacher was delighted. I was perplexed.

The fact that the children in both groups had mastered a significant segment of useable grammar became incidental. The specially designed instructional system had proved itself effective, but far more striking was the revelation of competition as a motivator. This was not a completely new discovery, however. As an educator, I have been taught and had taught others the importance of motivation. All the curricula I worked with stressed motivation. But this event brought the words to life. Motivation can propel students over high obstacles.

Eventually the enthusiasm of the children faded and they returned to their earlier ways. The experiment, however, provided more than one valuable lesson. In addition to the importance of competition, light was shed on children's need for success in whatever fashion—almost any fashion. Although in this case progress was not sustained, each child felt the satisfaction of accomplishment and knew that he was capable, in the right circumstances, of learning. Each child, in both groups, had a favorable experience impressed on his psyche.

The phenomenon of using special circumstances, atypical competition and uncommon attention to increase productivity, is well known in the industrial world. The unanticipated results from this study are reminiscent of the Hawthorne Effect. In the 1930s, experiments at a Western Electric plant showed that whenever management made changes in working conditions and systems, productivity went up. At first, management was mystified as to why minimal modifications brought dramatic results. Eventually they realized that the workers were responding not to improvements but to their employer's interest in them. This discovery fits well with the shopworn but veritable entreaty: Love me or hate me but don't ignore me.

Hawthorne Effects for underachievers are useful in implanting the notion that high levels of success are possible. Even a momentary achievement, properly exploited, can become a part of the foundation for restructuring your child's attitude.

The Underutilized Essential

As Jean Piaget implied, cognitive (thought processes) and affective (emotional processes) are two sides of the same coin. My own study and the classical Hawthorne Effect testify to the indivisibility of performance and emotion. They are never detached. They are forever enjoined. *The emotional side of performance, therefore, always affects the thinking side.* Professionals, researching in education and psychology, despite overwhelming evidence, sometimes are guilty of overlooking this inseparable relationship. As an old pro, I plead guilty to having made such an oversight in past endeavors. No longer.

The emotional side of the coin is given considerable deference by instructors and then ignored. The millions of underachievers confirm the problem.

As a parent, you can rectify the situation. You can structure the necessary emotional component that will make learning possible. Earlier, you were asked to stimulate your child's curiosity, to make your home conducive to learning, to build your child's self-esteem, and to loosen the anchors that held him back. Now add some more sail to get him going. *Strengthen the emotional aspect of learning.* Make him important. Talk with him and listen to him. Inject a healthy dose of praise for his efforts. Put greater effort into raising his confidence level and provide opportunities that will give him that exalted feeling of success. Combine all of your efforts into one strategy. Your approach will improve the attitude of your child.

Organize Your Strategies

The recipe for helping your child reach a desirable academic performance level calls for a stew of various essential ingredients. The components of this dish cannot be measured with the precision described in cookbooks. The concoction resembles, rather, that of the old-fashioned cook who had a "feel" for the right amount and threw some of the items into the pot. When asked for her recipe, she would respond, "Use a pinch of this and a dab of that. Not too much, mind you, just the right amount."

The bewildered beginner has considerable difficulty in determining the "too much" and the "right amount." The remedial recipe cannot be provided in specific quantities either. Your own observations (through trial and error) will have to determine when an ingredient is being used too much or too little. But remember: Include all incredients.

Praise Be Praised

"I don't have to show my appreciation for good work," snarls the administrator. "That's nonsense. Every time these employees receive a paycheck that's recognition that their efforts are satisfactory and appreciated. You don't coddle people. It spoils them."

As a consultant to various educational organizations, I've heard the aforementioned argument quite frequently. Poor work or poor attendance is always recognized quickly and noted with workers sometimes being called on the carpet. Exemplary performance and unexpected contributions are often overlooked.

"Well," said the administrator grudgingly, "tell her I said she did a nice job." The unexpected praise from higher up had a salutary effect on the woman in question but the extra efforts of many others, seemingly, went unnoticed. These workers continued to do their jobs nevertheless. But that's all most of them did—just what was expected. That little extra effort which would have saved the organization money, or increased productivity or sales, was absent.

"People work for a paycheck. Those with ambition work for a promotion. That's all there is to it." Numerous studies have proven this view a half-truth. Adults work for money but they require emotional rewards and satisfaction. So do children.

A five-minute lecture to a six- or ten-year-old on why he should do better in school is apt to be a time-waster and more. Many children will simply turn off. Studying becomes associated with harangue.

"If you don't learn your arithmetic, you won't be a rocket scientist," warns a parent. Most children would merely disregard such admonishments. Who wants to be that, anyway? In their imaginations, they can be anything they desire to be. Haul in the negative anchors and instead provide a modicum of praise.

A pinch of praise is just about the right amount. How much is that? It's similar to seasonings. Too little leaves the food flat. Too much can ruin a dish. The right amount leaves your child satisfied and eager to do more. Your judgment determines the quantity. Too little has no favorable effect. Too much loses its meaning. You taste food. You watch your child. You'll know.

If, as the Chinese philosophers said, a journey of a thousand miles begins with the first step, take that first step. Drop a compliment as your child sits down to do his schoolwork.

Don't emphasize it. Mix it in with other, neutral comments. He'll hear it. He'll remember it. He'll feel good about it. Wouldn't you?

"Let's get this assignment in order. You remember, just like the history lesson. You do it the same way. Decide what you have to do first. Find those capitals, right? Hey, look! You already found Albany. That's good work. I thought that would be difficult. Now, if you make a list of the states in one column you can put each capital in a column next to the states. See? That way you'll know which states you still have to do."

Praise some item to start. Find something, even if it's small. "That was a good word you selected for the sentence. Now, let's see what you can do with the others."

"Well, you did that difficult problem right. You're certainly making progress. You'll soon be able to get the others right, too."

A highly effective stratagem, if used judiciously, is the indirect method of praising. The criticism of the child, made to a third party but overheard, could be extremely detrimental. The opposite could be beneficial. You might praise the youngster to the third party when it is likely the child will overhear it. Again, just a pinch is enough.

"Yes, Billy is taking a keener interest in school now. You know what's interesting? He already does more and better work. I think he's on his way."

A casual favorable remark can be quite effective but a prepared script can be deadly. Avoid having your statements ready to use at a propitious moment. Children can sense insincerity. When the opportunity arises to praise your child, you'll have no difficulty choosing the words.

For educational purposes, divide your compliments into two categories. One concerns his physical and mental makeup. The other revolves around the challenges he faces and how well he accepts and completes them. You're dealing with a perfectly normal youngster, probably bright and perhaps very intelligent. These children are rarely credited with their true understanding of remarks and events. They may not respond in the same way as an adult, not because of lost nuances, but because of immature expressive power.

Assume that your child has an understanding commensurate with his age and mental capacity. Direct most of your praise toward his efforts and the resulting products rather than his inborn characteristics. Praise of his native abilities, if limited, will help at times, but this provides only a weak breeze against the sail. He may not be too successful in his efforts at this time, in which case he may doubt your judgment or even your honesty. "If I'm so good, why can't I do this?"

A more effective course is to direct your praise at his work, his improvements, and, when you truthfully can, his accomplishments. A satisfactorily finished product is far more of a convincer than references to his genetic strengths.

Compliments aimed at appearances, personality, clothes, and various possessions have the effect of making the recipient appreciate the speaker. They can be used with the learner, also, but should be minimized. The emphasis should be on performance. Sometimes you may be able to employ both.

"Billy, your teacher will like that model. It shows exactly

what you intended. I just knew you could do that kind of work.''

If Billy's teacher confirms the evaluation, he is on the road to utilizing his capabilities.

Use praise for:

1. Encouragement, not for increasing head size
2. A mild boost, not for providing a crutch
3. Recognition and reinforcement of progress
4. Countering earlier, deep-seated negatives

Confidence

If you think you can walk on a tight rope, you may be able to do it. If you're doubtful, you'd better not try. If you change the circumstances by placing a net under you, you could instill a degree of confidence. Convince your child he can do the work and, even if he slips sometimes while learning, a safety net that you have constructed will be in place to break his fall.

''I think you're ready for this kind of problem, Billy. You've learned everything up to this level, so you shouldn't have any difficulty. Anyhow, if you don't get it the first time, there'll be other opportunities.''

Confidence doesn't mean he expects to master a challenge immediately and without difficulty. Rather, it is the feeling that, given some reasonable effort and time, he will be able to learn the work facing him.

Confidence emanates from inside. You already know he can do the work by your earlier appraisals of his ability. He still has to be convinced.

The child, familiar with lack of achievement, cannot merely be told he is capable of better work. He must experience success, preferably in a series of related tasks. Confidence can be developed in increments. One step followed by a higher step, followed by still another step. Investors put their capital in companies with good track records. These companies have done it before, indicating that they can do it again. The learner, by succeeding in assignments, builds a track record of success.

He can't merely be told this with any degree of effectiveness. He develops the feeling by a combination of encounters with his environment. There's a good chance that the underachiever has had unsatisfactory experiences which have interfered with learning, but psychoanalysis is unnecessary. Incremental successful experiences will build a solid internal base and the negatives will eventually crumble. Success relegates past failures to history and lays the groundwork for continued achievement.

Success: The Healing Agent

A small success is similar to starting a campfire. If you can make one twig glow, you can kindle other twigs. A small flame can grow into a large fire. A small success can light other "learning twigs," bringing the desired outcome with the process. Parents must capitalize on "mini-positives."

Consider the case of ten-year-old Sharon who was assigned to write a composition relating to some pleasant summertime experience. Her fifth-grade teacher used the proven educational device of having the children report about an enjoyable event. All elementary children are familiar with writing tasks that say, "Tell about the most fun you had on your vacation (or over the holidays)." Each child then selects his own topic, one of special pleasure or significance to him.

Sharon had written about the family trip to Disney World, a subject certain to interest her peers. Sharon, however, as her mother knew too well, had never communicated with much success in writing. The child knew what she wanted to say but had difficulty in expressing her thoughts in a written format. After putting pen to paper she waited to hear her mother's verdict on this effort.

Reading slowly, her mother attempted to conceal her disappointment. Sharon had accepted the assignment with enthusiasm but the result was unsatisfactory. The mother had a choice of reactions.

"Now dear, this is not very good. You have to try harder. Sit down and start over. You want to succeed, don't you?"

Sharon wouldn't want to. She would just want out of the situation. The parent would have extinguished her fire, reinforced her negative views about writing, and offered nothing concrete to improve her skills.

A better reaction would be, "Dear, you certainly enjoyed our trip to Disney World. It comes through in your writing. You've made a good first draft. Let's think of ways to make it even better."

In the second example, the mother takes great care to keep the learning door open and avoid scuttling her child's effort. At the same time, she has not endorsed Sharon's unsatisfactory work.

Parents need not be professional writers to help their children. The example applies to all subjects. The parent's role is to guide her child toward improvement.

- Start with something done well or right.

"Your paper shows you really enjoyed the trip. So did I. Look at your last line. 'I hope there will be a next time.' That's good. That's really a fine way to end your paper."

- Involve the learner in evaluating the effort.

"Do you think you tried to get too much in? After all, we were there for two days. You can't describe everything in one report. Right?"

- Make a suggestion and be encouraging.

"What do you think about telling about just one exhibit? Which one do you think your classmates would be interested in most?"

"Good. Why don't you use the same opening and closing lines and concentrate on one item. You can do it. You're off to a fine start."

One effort will not elevate Sharon's writing skills to an "A" level but, over the course of time, she can hone the abilities she has. All subject matter may be approached similarly. Find something good and focus on it. Involve your child in evaluating his work and in planning improvements. Extirpate the negatives. If he's down on himself, remind him that the reason he's in school is to learn. If he already knew everything, he'd be the teacher. If most of his peers are doing better, list the areas where he is ahead or at least equal. Perhaps he has had a slow start or has been hindered by some unfortunate episode in the past, but he's turning things around. He'll soon catch up and you should be the one to convince him. He needs some successes, even small ones.

Encouragement

Your ongoing techniques should include gestures of approval. A finger circle signifying "OK," an acknowledging wave, an upraised thumb, a "V" sign are all pluses. Touching to show approval (and love) is almost a requirement. A playful tap, a light back slap or a hug far outweigh lectures in their degree of effectiveness. A positive reinforcer would be to accompany any of these gestures with a comment such as "Nice going," "Beautiful," or "You've got it." You can also nod, wink, and, above all, smile. When your child starts to turn things around, you won't have to do any of these things consciously. He'll read your approval as he does your love, in your mood, your voice, and your eyes.

Wrap-Up

The chapter on homework provided a rudimentary system for your child to approach assignments. Once he assimilates these step-by-step procedures, he will be able to expand and employ them without deliberate consideration. They will become part of his thinking processes in the same way he will or already has learned to master the art of bicycling. An accomplished rider needn't consciously instruct himself to maintain his balance by shifting his weight or to avoid obstacles by turning the handlebars. The subconscious mechanisms of the brain perform the required adjustments just as in other established skills and habits. Learning skills, once mentally digested, also will be automatically used as needed in problem solving. As the tasks become more advanced, the learning skills will become increasingly sophisticated.

The recipe for skill development includes six emotionally related ingredients. Each of these overlaps the others and the boundaries between them are usually obscure. The problem of the guiding parent is to provide a pinch of each and not to concern herself too much with specific categories and definitions. Call any facet what you will, but use it wisely to bring about the desired result.

Provide for:

Competition
Praise
Confidence-building
Successful experiences
Child involvement in decisions
Encouraged efforts

Skilled teachers are well aware of the best conditions for learning. They try to (1) make the material interesting at just the right level of difficulty; and (2) create a pleasant ambience for learning.

However, they will encounter some difficulties. Every child in the class is different. The possibility of catering to the diverse needs of every child present is unlikely. As a guiding parent, you can fill this gap to meet the needs of your child.

16

Listening
A Neglected Fundamental of Learning

A Skill to Be Learned

Probably nothing affects relationships more than the process of listening. Parents and their children are ideally situated for knowing each other, for mutual understanding of what "makes the other one tick." But a parent often complains, "I just don't understand that child!" Children agree.

There are, obviously, many breakdowns in communication within families. Social psychologists have long known that poor "interpersonal communication" results from a failure to listen. The message sent isn't being received as intended. A broadcast station can emit a strong signal but the television set or radio must be in operational condition and tuned in properly in order to receive it.

Listening

People feel the need to exchange information and thoughts. But the simple act of talking does not qualify as communication. The recipient of an idea may not agree with your message but the message itself must be decipherable.

The listening process for the parent of an underachieving child is near the top of essential learning elements. Just as a marriage counselor would be out of business if she couldn't address the necessity of communicating, your efforts to help your child would be stymied without adequate communication.

Certainly, *your child must listen to you.* But that's only one segment. *You must listen to your child.* You must avoid assuming that you know in advance precisely what your child has to say. Even if he has expressed his points earlier, there could be some subtle changes. Always listen carefully.

Listening is a learning skill that is absolutely vital to the student. Listening is usually and erroneously interpreted as a passive process. This misconception is the cause of many problems. Business transactions collapse, marriages dissolve, and children go astray because of one person's consistent failure to absorb another's signal. Listening requires the active processing of the thoughts and feelings underlying the words of the speaker.

Parent-Child Talk

Conversations between child and parent present many opportunities to bolster the underachiever. Set some rules for yourself to attain maximum benefits in this important area.

• Exchange views and avoid lectures.
"You can't see everything on television. Why don't you do your homework right after dinner and then you can relax while watching the shows before bedtime. What do you think?"

• Stay at his level with his interest.
"The program about the talking horse is funny. Of course, horses really can't talk, but notice that they use make-believe characters to say some important things?"

• Do not overdo the exchanges.
"Look how much time has gone by. I am really pleased by what you have to say. We'll talk again, soon."

• Disagree pleasantly.

"I don't know. That's not one of your better ideas and you do have some good ones. Maybe we ought to shelve that thought and look at it again some other time."

• Help him express his thoughts.

"Let's see if I have this right. You think I'm giving your brother more than his share. You want to review my decision. Right?"

• Reinforce your support for him even while making corrections.

"That was a shoddy effort and you know it. You are capable of much better work. Let's start all over. I'll be here if you need me."

• Build his self-esteem and confidence while discussing other matters.

"A C+ is much better than a C–. We just started this new program and you're already making progress. Arithmetic really isn't difficult. I think you're ready to try the word problems."

• Show your love but vary your means of expressing it.

"I understand. When things go wrong for you, I feel the pain too."

Conversations may produce desired results. They may be unplanned, scheduled quality time or an aspect of homework. These conversations between your child and yourself will help to solidify his feeling of belonging to the family. He wants to be part of this group. Include him. If there is a spouse and older children at home, be sure they do, too.

Use these talks as a means of getting at a problem. For example, if you sense a feeling of insecurity or frustration over a weakness, observe "in passing" that everyone has some frailty. Relate stories about people he knows. Use yourself as an illustration. Discuss other people's setbacks and how they were overcome.

The bonds between your offspring and yourself can be cemented by direct talks. All children can learn through these exchanges. The underachiever may have a longer road to travel

but including him in suitable discussions will reinforce and
raise his self-value.

Raising the Attention Level

Working with your child during his homework assignments
and holding periodic conferences will afford you the opportunity to learn about and improve his level of attention.

Watch your child's eyes. You will know instantly whether
he is attentive. What is their direction? They may be focused on
something else such as a bug on a window sill. Yes, he hears
you, but incompletely. He may be thinking of other things
which at that moment are more important or more interesting to
him than your words. Your voice may have been relegated to
background noise. If so, his eyes will have a faraway look.

Watch his gestures and movements. He may demonstrate
rapt attention by his facial expressions which become fixed as
his eyes look into yours. He may turn slightly but still be
listening carefully. Nothing else is commanding his attention
and his eyes are clear.

He may tilt his head slightly which suggests he is evaluating
your message. An almost imperceptible nod may indicate
agreement or understanding or both.

His fingers may stroke part of his face or a pencil or other
object. If he is attending to this activity, he is probably just
waiting for you to finish. He is listening but there is little
acceptance or he is bored. In his view, he has heard it all before.
If, however, he seems oblivious to his movements, such as
stroking or doodling, he is concentrating on the conversation.

Pause briefly and watch his reaction. If he is not aware of
silence, you've lost him. If, after a second or two, he looks
directly at you with a muscular contortion that asks, "Well? Go
on," you have him. He's been listening, with comprehension.

If he demonstrates mixed reactions, you can capture his
attention by frequent pauses and a sudden question. Avoid
asking, "Are you following me?" You want him to understand
your expectations—that he is listening. Instead, ask a question
that assumes he is immersed in thought about the conversation.
"What do you think, Jim? Can it be done that way?" By

elucidating an occasional comment from the child, you involve him in the two-way exchange of thoughts.

Avoid scolding him for inattentiveness. "Jim! Are you listening?" You may interrupt a reverie by startling him but you've gained little. Instead, apply some evaluative criteria to bring him around. Ask yourself some questions:

1. Am I sermonizing instead of instructing? The sermon is fixed with minimal interruptions. Instruction on the other hand is a give-and-take procedure that changes as the learner progresses.
2. Is he participating in the dialogue or am I monopolizing the conversation? A two-way street must be in place.
3. Am I speaking in conversational tones or is my voice harsh and forbidding? I don't want him to press his mute button.
4. Have I gone beyond his attention span? He may not be able to listen carefully for long periods of time.
5. Is the timing right? Is there something else due or going on? Dinner? A favorite television program? A waiting friend?
6. Have I gone beyond his comprehension? Did I lose him? Did I forget to hold his attention and evaluate his interest and progress?

These frequent parental errors are easily correctable if you include the child in the exchange. Eliminate diatribes. Create conversation. Both of you talk. Both of you listen.

Your child can sense being ignored. If *his* message goes unheard, he may adopt a defensive strategy to bolster his own need for security. He may retreat into a protective shell of silence. The child, overly wrapped in his own thoughts and in his own private world, may grow into a failed adult. This can be prevented.

Listening: A Learning Skill

Limited listening skills alone may account for a child's less-than-expected academic achievement. The mind of a

member of an audience may drift without anyone being aware
of it. A speaker may not capture the complete attention of his
audience, but virtually all participants will join in the applause
and no one will detect the wandering mind. A student in a
classroom, however, may suffer severe losses from repeated
interruptions of pupil-teacher communications.

The mind of a student, at all levels, will wander periodically,
but successful learners will be able to assemble pieces they
have heard and fill in the gaps, or, failing that, get information from a friend or textbook. The elementary school
pupil who has not mastered the art of listening may have a
damaged rung on his learning ladder. An essential step in the
learning process is missing and he may not know what to do
about it.

The child must understand that listening is an integral part of
communication, not only with his parents, siblings, other
relatives, and friends, but with his teacher. He must learn to
follow her explanations and instructions. A good teacher
repeats all important information. A poor listener strikes out
anyway.

Few schools assign adequate homework involving effective
listening skills, or even deal with it directly in classrooms. The
learning-to-learn concept, of which listening is a basic segment, is generally neglected by the educational system. An
active, discriminating listener has a far better chance for
success, in school and elsewhere. You can help your child
improve this skill.

• Read a story aloud—one that is a bit beyond your child's
reading level. A newspaper report or magazine article will do.
Have him tell you what he heard or have him write it out if he
can.

How much meaning did he grasp and how accurate is his
version? Depending on his age, you can ask for a simple
summary or a full outline of essential points. Have the child
understand that you expect his version to agree with the
original material.

• After visitors have left, have your child tell you what he
heard that might have impressed him. Discuss it. Perhaps a

neighbor's cat just had a litter—how many kittens and what colors? Does Uncle Bob's new job seem as exciting as he described—and what does a sales manager do?

• Emphasize listening with discrimination. Could that television program about killing elephants for ivory have been handled in another manner? What was boring, poorly presented, or omitted? What issues were presented fairly? Did the narrator use any "big words" or good descriptive phrases?

Levels of Listening

Listening encompasses more than the obvious. A person says something; a second party hears and deciphers the meaning. Once your child, through practice and adult direction, has learned the rudiments, the skill should be carried to a higher level.

How a statement is presented or even enunciated on television, for instance, may be as important as the words used. You can't always latch onto a good example to help your child understand the subtleties, but you can create your own illustrations. For instance, a TV anchorman was reporting on a foreign government's response to a murder of innocent civilians. His script probably read, "They say there will be an immediate and full-scale investigation of the atrocity." If the anchorman was unbiased and merely reporting the news, he could have concluded with that statement. However, he couldn't resist some editorial changes. He enunciated "They say" with such emphasis that it contrasted sharply with the remaining words in the statement. Not satisfied, he hesitated, and then added a skeptical "We'll see."

For your own illustrations, you can select topics in your child's area of interest.

"Your teacher likes your reports to be in blue ink." The statement, just an acknowledgment of fact, is clear. Don't use black or blue-black—use blue.

You can demonstrate how meanings can be altered without changing a word. Use the news commentator's technique.

Explain carefully to your child that, for the purposes of illustration, you are distorting your own view about his teacher. Then repeat the statement about how she prefers blue ink but emphasize, with a bit of sarcasm in your voice, "Your teacher." Now the sentence implies something more. Any other teacher wouldn't care about the color of ink used, but this one does. Very petty.

Your child, through such exercises, will be led to understand that listening requires more than just hearing and accepting words at face value. The point may be made by practice and the practice may be made into a family game. Choose sentences from newspapers, magazines, or ordinary conversation. Have the players change the intended meaning by varying the modes of expression. You can have winners, if you like, by voting for the best distortion. You may also have a player add a comment to modify the intent of a statement.

After a sentence, add:

"So he says."
"Believe it or not."
"Here we go again."
"Really?"

Preface a sentence with:

"Get this."
"His words, not mine."
"For the record, he said."
"He said, with a straight face . . ."

The auditory aspects of listening should be combined with visual intake and supported by cognitive interpretation. In most situations, a radio being a notable exception, the listener sees the person speaking. Visual clues can be added to the words and intonations to gain a fuller understanding of the message.

Turn on a television news show and turn off the sound. Use the speaker's body language to determine his sincerity, emphasis, and truthfulness. For instance, folded arms may indicate defensiveness, or leaning forward with an extended index finger may reveal aggressiveness.

Observe the speaker's eyes for signs about mood or interest

or study facial changes of color which may indicate embarrassment or doubt. Tears show many things, including remorse or helplessness.

As your child becomes more sophisticated in listening, he will gain an improved understanding of his teachers. By combining analytical listening and careful observation, he'll be able to anticipate the subject matter covered in tests, including some actual questions, and will be able to follow her instructional direction.

This is important; this is not.

This is the information I want regurgitated.

This is where you must think for yourself.

The listening game will open up new avenues for your child. He will not only become a better student but he will learn to apply the same listening principles outside of school and into adult life. He will find it advantageous to decipher the meaning behind words actually spoken. This skill is usually referred to as "reading between the lines." He will become skilled in understanding and using metaphors and will become proficient in interpreting words used to conceal real meanings.

Wrap-Up

Listening skills should be learned early for application in school and throughout adult life.

Listening is a key but underutilized learning tool.

Listening to the words alone and ignoring clues from sight, tone, expression, and the possible intent of the speaker may distort the listener's understanding of concepts and information.

Listening is part of communication which travels in two directions simultaneously. Both parties must speak *and* listen.

Children can learn listening skills by attending an event and then explaining whatever transpired.

Children learn the basics of listening rather readily and, if the practice continues, become quite accomplished in detecting implicit meanings.

Listening skills can be employed to make a speaker more

convincing, a salesperson more productive, and a teacher more effective.

Listening-skill development is a means to increase the child's vocabulary, sharpen his analytical ability, enhance his memory, and improve his perception. Learning is never a singular process.

17

Guiding the Divergent Thinker

The Realization of Potential

"There is only one real solution to this problem," explained the teacher. "Just look around before you enter a tunnel or cross a bridge. You'll see many cars with just the driver or maybe one passenger. This has to stop. Each car should ideally hold four or five people during rush hour, but there should be a law requiring a minimum of three."

Vince and the other sixth-graders in the advanced group duly noted the teacher's words in their looseleaf books. The lesson was entitled "Urban Problems" and New York was being cited as an example. The question now being discussed centered on traffic jams during rush hours on business days.

"What else might help?" asked the instructor.

"Buses," volunteered a girl.

"Yes. Mass transportation could help. Why don't more people use buses and trains?"

"They're not convenient," noted a youngster. "You have to be able to get to them. For many people, that means driving to a station."

"What's wrong with that?"

"It takes time," answered the boy.

"You have to meet a bus or train schedule," added another pupil.

"You need a place to park," a third student commented.

A teacher is pleased when his class comes alive and this one was buzzing. Some of the children were chatting among themselves. A visiting supervisor might have considered the class unruly but Mr. Jenkins knew that the little scattered discussions were on the topic. Whenever he started to speak, the room became quiet, a certain sign that he was in control.

"Okay. What else can cut down the traffic jams?"

"Richard?"

"Build more tunnels and bridges," the excited boy exclaimed. He was sure he had found the best solution.

"Why don't we do that, class?"

"Money!" three students thundered.

"No place to put them," Robert added.

"Isn't there any room between the existing bridges and tunnels, Robert?" asked the teacher.

"Yes, but there's no place to build access roads. It wouldn't help to have more bridges if you couldn't get on and off them easily. You would just be moving your traffic jams to another place and . . ."

"Hold it, Robert. I think you might find some areas where it would be practical. If it had been planned, the Hudson River could have been spanned at the World Financial Center or Battery Park. The costs, though, would probably have been prohibitive."

The teacher's comments triggered an idea in the mind of Dawn who had, until now, been quiet.

"Use ferries!" she shouted excitedly. "They wouldn't cost too much."

"Good thinking," Mr. Jenkins acknowledged. "That happens to be one of the possibilities now being considered. Any other ideas? No? All right. Maybe you'll think of some later.

"Now let's look at some of the other urban problems."

Mr. Jenkins then read from prepared material about airplanes circling the crowded skies above Kennedy and

LaGuardia airfields waiting for their turn to land, the growing pollution caused by vehicles, the loss to businesses of customers unwilling to navigate the crowded highways, the exodus of many corporate headquarters and the ongoing high unemployment rate among some of the city's minority citizens.

"For next Monday, I want you to select a problem and, if you're daring, maybe two, and tell us what you would do to help solve it. Make your solutions realistic. No aliens, please."

The class laughed. Lance, in an earlier related assignment, had suggested an agreement with UFOs to transfer cargo instead of using 18-wheelers.

The children made their notes and left the room. Many continued talking about urban problems in the hallways as they moved toward their next class.

Vince had his own thoughts. "Select a problem, and, if you're daring, maybe two," the teacher had instructed. One? Two? Why not more? One solution fits all, thought Vince. Worth a try.

Relating Disparate Elements

"What do you think, Mom? Will it work?"

"I don't know, dear," Vince's mother answered, enunciating each word. She was looking at the plan her child had drawn up and thinking intently. Her voice understood the responsibility of answering Vincent while her mind was busy analyzing the document.

"All right, where's the summary?"

"Right here," Vincent answered enthusiastically.

"Let's see. You're going to put a huge airfield in northwest New Jersey. Why there?"

"Every area surrounding New York is crowded. Even if you expanded Newark's airport, you would be overlapping New York's air space."

"Then you would construct a high-speed monorail into Manhattan using existing rail lines?"

"Right."

"Using Japanese designers?"

"No. Americans could do it," explained Vince proudly.

"You would build bus highways and rail lines to the airfield?"

"Right. There would be limited stops and each would have a modern parking facility.

"Commuters from North Jersey could then use the new airfield and it would also serve the needs of flights from other parts of the country," Vince explained.

"You've lowered the traffic jam on the ground and in the air somewhat and I guess limited the vehicle pollution. I suppose that might encourage companies to stay in New York. But what's that got to do with minority employment?"

"It's a whole new opportunity for young people. Construction pays good."

"Pays well."

"Right. You can train willing people to learn these jobs and the apprenticeship is short. A few months, a year, maybe two. Even the helpers get paid—well. People who are already in construction will take some jobs leaving their positions open for others."

"Well, this isn't pie in the sky. The incentive is real," added his mother. "But what happens when the project is completed? All of these people lose their jobs?"

"No, no," came Vince's excited response. "If it works, other cities will be building the same thing. They'll need some of the workers from this project because they're now experienced. And don't forget the maintenance on this thing. That will employ many people."

Vince's mother swallowed her skepticism. "And how do you expect to pay for all this?"

Vince was ready. "It can be built with bond money and the bonds can be paid off by the riders as part of their fare." He didn't add his thoughts on the additional tax revenues from increased business and a higher rate of employment.

"Well, Mom?"

"Yes. Turn it in. See what Mr. Jenkins thinks. After all, it's just the beginning of an idea."

"Right."

Vince's 'right' repeated itself in her mind. She watched as he happily gathered together the maps and demographic charts—his supporting evidence. He's 11, she reflected. What's he going to be like when he's 30?

No Longer an Underachiever

While Vince's mother did not help in creating the youngster's plan, she played, as usual, the role of friendly critic. She understood her child's propensity to think differently than his peers on many topics and his need to formulate and express his own concepts. Children such as Vince, stymied in their efforts to be creative and channeled into inflexible conventional paths, could easily become frustrated and possibly become underachievers. Vince had been one of these children. His grades had always been above average but his efforts in school had always been measured. He had learned to do exactly what the teacher required and no more. His limited endeavors were brought about by negative experiences. He had found that going a step beyond expectations was accepted but that his conclusions had to fit a predetermined pattern. Very often, his conclusions didn't match those expected by the teacher and were usually set aside as being incorrect or irrelevant. Vince assumed that something was wrong with his mind and stifled his urges to search out many possibilities on an assignment.

Vince's mother was always aware that her son was not typical of boys his age. For a time she couldn't identify the problem. She did watch his schoolwork carefully and came to the realization that her child sometimes interprets events differently than most people and feels compelled to pursue new and untried approaches to resolve problems. She became aware that his internal compulsion clashed with his external environment, especially in school. Through trial-and-error procedures, she helped Vince understand both himself and others. He learned to present his views in a fashion others could comprehend. Once he overcame the doubt about himself and was free from the frustration he had previously experienced, Vince climbed the academic ladder. By the sixth grade, he was admitted to an accelerated class where his work was recognized as being outstanding.

During the construction phase of Vince's tr
project, his mother had suggestions and aske
designed to make him think, particularly about possible omissions. She knew children learn best by exploring, manipulating,
and decision making. She helped to shape the project by her
careful queries. At one point, for instance, she had noted, "You
have some good highway maps of New Jersey and New York.
Did you get your railroad and demographic maps yet?" Vince
hadn't thought of getting the additional maps and didn't know
what "demographic" meant, but decided to find out.

"While you're at the library, why don't you check to see if
there have been some recent magazine articles on modern rail
transportation? If you can't get a librarian with enough time to
help you, I'll go with you next time."

"Do you think it's a good idea to show distances on your
routes so someone can get a feel for the project?"

"Do you think that paper will tear readily? Have you tried
the art supply store? Maybe they can recommend something."

Vince's plan was praised by his teacher, graded with an
"A" and displayed on the bulletin board. His classmates
appreciated his blending of colors, his clearly marked routes,
and the time spent on creating his work. Vince's teacher saw
more in the effort; that is, the young child's ability to combine
seemingly unrelated areas into one subject.

"Look, Claude. It was drawn up by a kid in my
enrichment class. You know, kids with a lot on the ball.
Anyhow, he's got the lines penciled in, the routes, the
mileage, the airfield, the . . . Why won't it work? What
do you mean 'too many pieces?' Oh. No one would listen?
I see. Well, thanks anyhow. I thought you might be
interested. Lunch? Sure."

The Divergent Mind

The need to learn is common with all children but some feel
compelled to follow additional impulses. The child who feels
driven to pursue his own particular yearnings, who diverges
from the mainstream, is charging a hurricane made up of the
conventional or convergent thinking majority. The child who

pursues his own predilections irrespective of the desires of others, without guidance, faces the possibility of being blown away. These children, too, are individuals. They differ from the majority but differ from each other too. They fail to fall within prearranged boundaries that simplify their characteristics and make them easy to identify. Their behavior, even when they are properly labeled, is unpredictable.

They, the concept weavers of the human species, are not always understood. Sometimes, to escape the herd instinct of others, they travel infrequently used highways or where there are no roads at all. As children, many are academic under-achievers. If the talents of these youngsters are not cultivated early, potentially monumental contributions may be lost. There is no way to calculate how many Freuds or Curies or Hawkings there might have been.

Because of the support of his parents, Thomas Edison became a great inventor. His school kicked him out. His teachers decided that he was unfit for school and they were right. He was not well suited for the prescribed, narrow, slow-moving pace of the school's program. His curriculum was the world.

Young Tom's parents played a vital role in his life. They nurtured his inquisitiveness and creativity—both in their own way. His mother, Nancy, as much of a disciplinarian as his teachers, kept him in line. Her emphasis was on practical work. Sam, his father, let the boy explore the world on his own. Tom's interests drifted toward mechanics, chemistry, and business. His contributions to the fields of economics and electromechanics are legendary.

Your Child?

Definitions differ, but for our purposes, divergent intelligence refers to creative *thinking,* which includes innovative concept formation or revolutionary mechanical arrangements. The final product may be offered in words, blueprints, or mathematics. Artistic creativity, recognized by schools, is something different, a specialized talent. Mozart, for instance, organized innovative arrangements and created unsurpassed compositions, but within one artistic field. Jefferson, on the other hand, had original or divergent concepts, and his startling "self-evident" truths, in his strong prose, transformed society. Some people are blessed, or perhaps burdened, with both creative thinking and artistic talent. Leonardo da Vinci, who was propelled by an insatiable curiosity, is an example. The line between divergent thinking and artistic creation can be at times blurred.

This work is concerned not with the geniuses cited but lesser intellects who nevertheless have divergent characteristics. All people have occasional nonconformist thoughts or ideas that appear to be original. Most people have some of the qualities attributable to innovative thinkers. You should not, as a responsible parent, assume that an episode here or there or a periodic burst of independent activity defines your child as being different and creative. Nearly every child has an element of divergence in his makeup.

Parents almost always like to have bright children but sometimes are uncertain of how to handle situations with their child that do not follow the norm. Many parents would refrain from encouraging their child to be different unless the difference was in developing a valuable talent or demonstrating leadership or scholarship. The question arises rather consistently as to whether parents should encourage or restrain differences from others in their children. There are some considerations.

The mere thinking, saying, or doing something different does not, in and of itself, imply something positive. Many cults, for instance, suggest a different way of life. Nonconformity cannot always be equated with offering a valuable contribution. Immoral behavior, dangerous acts, or lawbreaking are nonconformities. A parent must call on her own reasoning and experiences to consider whether a difference is advantageous or a problem.

Differences from adult standards of dress, hair, and speech styles are pseudo nonconformities. The youngsters are actually conforming to a code established by some of their peers. They're exhibiting nothing original and are not improving society. They're not necessarily hurting society either. Their differences do not meet the criteria for divergent thinking used in this book.

Inventing new ideas or even organizations can be meaningless. Would you be interested, for example, in purchasing an electric eggshell-cracker or making a monetary contribution to the Society for the Clothing of Naked Animals?

Parental Role: Identify and Assist

The personalities of these exceptional folk, the divergent thinkers, follow no prescribed format; they may be outgoing or shy, likable or defensive, energetic or lethargic. They can't be identified by their appearance. Their choice of clothing may be bizarre or conservative; they may be dapper or stodgy. Brief encounters generally reveal little. A person must get to know them. Parents have this opportunity.

The divergent thinking child will have some of the following characteristics in varying degrees. The child may intuitively realize that others do not share all of his interests, concerns, or stratagems. If he adjusts to his real-life situations as they evolve, and if he does well in school, there is no cause for special parental attention. If you have determined that your child is an underachiever and that divergent thinking is a likely cause, then your intervention is obligatory.

Consider that this child must understand himself and others around him and see some way to accommodate his differences. If such understandings are grasped in elementary grades, the child will have no more difficulty accepting the dissimilarities between himself and his friends than a child who is much taller or brighter than the rest of his peers.

Nonconformist in Thought and Private Actions

"Mom, I don't think the teacher is right. She said scientists are open-minded and always looking for facts."

"Isn't that true, dear?"

"No, not always. Sometime they're just like everyone else. If something bothers them, they yell before thinking."

"Really? You better think that through."

"I did. Remember those books you gave me? Look how scientists jumped on Louis Pasteur and Emmanuel

Velikofsky. They didn't want facts. They didn't want change.''

"You do have a point, but you're jumping to conclusions too quickly. You're going to need more information. An isolated case here and there is not sufficient evidence. What are you going to answer if the question is used in a test?''

"I don't know. What should I do?''

"I can't tell you that. If you disagree with the teacher on a test, how will she mark it?''

"Wrong.''

"Then you lose.''

"What can I do?''

"Try a different strategy. Don't wait for the test. Go to the teacher and tell her you've been thinking about what she said. Mention Pasteur because he was right. Omit Velikofsky. His theories are still quite controversial.''

"It's not his theories but how scientists reacted that I'm talking about.''

"All right. Tell the teacher that you are finding the subject interesting, which you are, and that you have questions about some scientists, which you have. Tell her you would like to do some library research on the topic if she would help you. If you find anything that she thinks the class ought to know, you'll make a report.''

"Hey, great. It might be a good topic for a class debate. I'll see her tomorrow. Thanks, Mom.''

The parent in the story was confronted with a typical reaction from a divergent-thinking child. They may or may not disagree openly but they notice something is wrong, something they can't readily accept. To compound the difficulty, the undigestible morsel may be on any issue.

Children learn to dampen thoughts that digress from the mainstream. Many realize that challenging an authority figure can be injurious to their stability. If parents confirm the suppression, they're allowing their child's growth to stagnate. Parents are continually faced with enigmas and decisions. There are so many wrong ways to do things, and so many wrong signals that can be sent:

''Dear, the teacher knows what she's talking about. That's why she's there.''

''You may be right but it's better to go along. Don't start trouble.''

''Stand up for your principles. Tell your teacher she's wrong.''

The parent doesn't have to have a ready answer for anything that might arise. ''Let me think about that'' is a perfectly acceptable response, providing the parent does give the question thought and then addresses the query within a short time period.

Elementary school issues are not necessarily as earthshaking as a San Francisco quake, but they are important in developing the cognitive structure for future decisions. The mother in the ''Scientists are always open-minded'' account refused to provide the definitive answer for her child. Instead, she maneuvered the youngster into reexamining his hasty conclusion. She noted that for purposes of tests, the major criterion for grades, the teacher would expect her answer to be the correct one. The mother then suggested a viable approach for this child to follow which has applications for education, commerce, and industry. *Open the door to further study without being negative, volunteer to do most of the work, and involve all parties in the conclusion to be drawn.*

Instead of antagonizing the ''expert'' or playing the role of an obsequious sheep, the child was given an opportunity to learn, to validate, or alter his own impressions, to nurture a divergent hunch and to work within the established framework without squelching his own impulses.

Abhors Convention and Tradition

Barbara was going through a stage during her upper elementary school years when she enjoyed challenging accepted activities. ''Why do we have to do that?'' Sometimes parents must take the position when they answer and enforce ''Because I want it done.'' Other questions require more of an explanation. The reasons behind the actions may be obscure, but the act has become part of the culture. Children, especially the divergent-thinking ones, have difficulty accepting this.

In the play, *Fiddler on the Roof,* Tevye, the Jewish milkman in Czarist Russia, when unable to provide a logical answer to a probing mind, responds "Tradition!" That's why they do what they do. It's tradition.

If your child is persistent, even with an acceptable voice, you may find it tiresome singing the same response to varied questions. Instead, unless you know the answers, involve the child in finding the answers.

Going through a book on manners found in the attic of her house, Randi came across a notation that gentlemen, escorting ladies, walk on the curb side. The book offered no explanation, so Randi asked her father.

"That came into being when streets were unpaved and a fast-moving wagon crossing a puddle might cause a splash. The idea, naturally, was that the man would shield the woman."

The idea appealed to Randi.

"Doesn't sound fair," said her younger brother.

Randi, watching a television show, turned to her mother and asked why people, especially men, greeted each other by shaking hands.

"Find out," she was advised.

She announced her discovery at dinner the following night. "The tradition goes back to ancient times. When two men met, they extended their right hands to show they weren't holding a sword or dagger."

Finding "reasonable" explanations usually satisfies the questioning, creative mind. In Randi's home the family developed a game of "Why do we do this?" Some answers were obvious or readily available. Others seemed veiled. One of these, again, resulted from watching television. In an old movie about live theater, an actress is stricken and can't perform. Everyone on the program agreed that the show must go on. Randi wanted to know why. "It's a show business tradition," offered her father.

Randi rejected the explanation.

"Because the theater manager has sold all the tickets and doesn't want to give the money back," her mother volunteered.

Randi was satisfied.

Parents need not be scholars nor always send their children hunting for reasons that tend to be nebulous. They must, however, convince their children that society, does, in fact, revolve around convention and tradition. Sometimes there are good and useful reasons for the things we do. Sometimes the reasons are rather vague. Children are entitled to their own opinions but, unless these conventions and traditions are harmful to someone, children should be taught to respect or at least tolerate them.

Imaginative

In a group of young children, one or a few tend to be the organizers of games. Some little ones seem to be able to improvise as needed and suggest endless variations to old procedures.

Not uncommonly, these same youngsters are the ones who write prose or poetry and create their own newspapers. They frequently include editorials in the publication of their newspapers that present new and different views from those held by their friends. Jill and Beth published "Kidstuff" without help. A young Thomas Edison published a newspaper on a train, doing all of the tasks himself.

Parents should encourage imaginative efforts but caution children that their products, whatever they may be, must be accepted to be successful. "You've got to make a newspaper people will buy. You can't put in anything you feel like. People must want to read your writing."

Original Concepts

No one knows whether an original concept is original. Did its promotor read about it some years earlier, or is it a combination of ideas others have proffered? If so, is it a unique combination?

The unbridled imagination of the developed thinker allows him to proceed in oblique directions and his flexibility enables him to retreat from a dead end and try other avenues. His ability to relate disparate elements in an extraordinary way may generate ideas that, in the form presented, may be considered original. Vince, who never even visited New York, tried to solve some of that city's problems.

Mainstream thinking usually focuses on one issue at a time. Related aspects are set aside for another time. People such as Vince try to relate all the pieces and create a mosaic, one grand solution. Vince's parents allowed him to proceed with his assignments as he wished but offered suggestions on items to consider and information to research. They cautioned him about expecting unqualified acceptance of his ideas.

Timing and Usefulness

The parent of a divergent thinker is challenged to go beyond having the child understand himself and others. The parent should view the child's differences as a special thinking talent and not an albatross. The child should be treated much like a youngster with outstanding athletic or musical ability. His ideas need to be valued and evaluated. He should learn to present them in a manner that will make them welcome by others.

A penchant for iconoclasm could cause the divergent-thinking child to become estranged from the group in the early grades. This may be followed by withdrawal, belligerency, or indifference. This child must face a world that has initially resisted his new ideas. Unless he has been prepared for the realistic encounters that will come, his creative fire could be doused quickly by the waters of misunderstanding. The child should learn in his earliest years that the fruition of creative thought is largely dependent on timing. The nimble mind will select propitious moments for unique and original presentations.

Ideas or inventions must have utility and either replace or add something philosophical or tangible to society. The timing must be right. At the time of their proposal or unveiling they may seem unrealistic to the first audience. The vast majority of people can only operate within a familiar, narrow, and plainly visible world. The divergent mind sees the possibilities that most of us miss. But telling us about their ideas is insufficient. The majority of people are neither short-sighted nor stupid.

Their learning is pyramidical; new concepts fit comfortably on top of the structure already in place. Critical and/or logical thinking is not a component of most curricula.

The divergent thinker's mind can go in any direction—reach out to grab a concept on the side, or return to the starting point to begin again. The innovator has multidirectional sight. Many traditionalists only have a clear view of the road ahead. Other thinking is just myopic.

Remember these quotes?

"The telephone is a highly interesting toy."

"The automobile may have some useful purpose but can never replace the horse."

"If God wanted man to fly, He would have given him wings."

"Women vote? Who will tell single women how to vote?"

"The only organizations that will be able to afford computers are the federal government, the army, and a few giant corporations. It's not a business to enter."

Parental Help

- Parents should get involved by encouraging their child to present his views even if, on first hearing, they appear to lack value.
- The child should be given a chance to retreat, reflect, and re-present.
- The child should be asked how he arrived at each point and be given adequate time to modify his reasoning as well as his response. This practice requires patience, which is not everyone's forte, but that doesn't make it less valuable. The more creative a thinker the child is, the more patience is required.
- The parent must attempt to answer even bewildering questions. It is certainly permissible to ask the child to explain or rephrase his query. If stumped over a point, the parent should tell the child. At the same time, the youngster should be encouraged to continue with his thinking.

- The questions of a child may indicate a journey through a make-believe world. Parents should avoid inhibiting his imagination. He is entitled to his fantasies. Many books, plays, inventions, and concepts were conceived in daydreaming.
- The parent should help the divergent-thinking child recognize that:
  - His thinking will often differ from others—be they his peers or adults—throughout his life.
  - His efforts may be sporadic, with periods of high productivity. When he becomes inspired, he must work at that time. He can't plan inspiration days on a calendar. However, schoolwork must usually follow a schedule. He must do the best he can on an ongoing basis.
  - Teachers and parents are sometimes wrong. Even brilliant people make mistakes, but tact in discussion is a necessity for a successful outcome.
  - He may find that standard procedures available are inadequate for his purposes and may have to create new methodologies to reach his goal.
  - Not all questions have correct or incorrect answers. Some problems lend themselves to multiple solutions.
  - The results of his efforts may surprise even himself.
  - The more radical the solution to a problem, the more care he must exercise in offering it to others. People tend to resist changing accepted beliefs.
  - Any departure from the status quo in a serious matter is disturbing to people who are comfortable with the existing arrangement. Even ''experts'' may be threatened by innovative ideas if they are not fully versed in new approaches.
  - Being right or more nearly right than others does not guarantee acceptance of an idea.
  - His recommendations to solve a problem could cause other problems. The law that ''for every action there is an equal and opposite reaction'' applies to more than physics.
  - He will continue to face people with less productive

imaginations, even though they are intelligent in other areas and hold important positions.

- He must view his own work with extreme caution. Being different cannot be equated with being right.
- He must test the accuracy and practically of his concepts prior to an open presentation.
  1. Discuss them with a knowledgeable, friendly colleague. Flaws in thinking may show up and corrections can be made.
  2. Be his own devil's advocate and attack the work in part and as a whole.
  3. Play the role of juror and evaluate his defense of the critic's barbs.
  4. Allow the idea to remain dormant for a while and then look at it through fresh eyes.
- To gain acceptance of his thesis in a working group he must:
  1. Introduce it with a simple overview.
  2. Present one segment of his proposition at a time in a logical manner.
  3. Couch his concept in familiar terms.
  4. Give his associates credit for its formulation, whether or not they actually made significant contributions. Such phrases as "We decided . . ." and "Our plan . . ." are effective ways of gaining acceptance of a concept. People will be far more amenable to any change that enables them to share the credit for having conceived it. If the concept is good and the timing is right, instead of being rebuffed, the originator will receive most of the recognition due him.

Wrap-Up

Schools do little about a child with a high degree of divergent intelligence, but you as a parent can make up for the educational system's shortcoming. Bear in mind that:

1. All normal children have some degree of divergent intelligence.

2. Even if your child is a divergent thinker, he is still an individual, still unique. You must adapt any program to fit his particular needs.
3. Your child has all the needs all children have. None of these should be ignored.
4. The divergent-thinking child needs to understand himself and others and how these others view him and interpret his ideas.

18

The Art of Test-Taking

Common Problem

"Wally's no good at tests," observes his classmate. His mother, Adele, a teacher, recognizes the significance of the statement immediately. Wally, introduced earlier, can, for reasons unknown at the moment, learn in class and at home, but slips badly in demonstrating what he's learned under testing conditions. Several explanations are possible, but Adele is not sure which is the right one. Instead of guesses and hasty conclusions, she institutes a system of analysis that will identify the reason behind her son's lack of success. Once she has established the cause she will be able to utilize effective remedial measures.

No Escape

Tests are an integral part of our educational program throughout the elementary, secondary, and college years. Test results are used for review and as identification of weak areas as well as for determining marks and group placement.

Colleges use tests for entrance examinations and in their degree programs.

Examinations permeate the world of the military, commerce, industry, civil service, and professional organizations. Tests are usually mandatory to become a police sergeant, a real estate broker, a lawyer, a barber, or a certified public accountant. The levels are different but the principles are the same. Careers are regulated and determined by test performance. Many people spend critical years in the workplace avoiding tests and, thereby, curtail their advancement opportunities.

Test-taking should be mastered when learning is easiest— while the child is young. The schools will certainly provide many tests along the way. You, as the guiding parent, unless the child has a natural affinity for taking tests, can help your child become a test-taking craftsman.

The student competent in taking tests has a distinct advantage over the rest of the competition. The student who fares poorly in examinations may cease to be a student at the legal dropout age. Finally, test-taking skills will ultimately determine a student's degree of academic success.

Test Mismanagement

Inadequacy in test-taking can have many causes. Your task, as guider, is to determine why your child cannot perform well on tests. Knowing your child, you may already understand the reason intuitively or have had some indication as you began the program. Some confirmation or new discoveries might help.

Steps:

1. Simulate a test based on the child's schoolwork and observe him. In reality, the pressure is absent, but some clues may be apparent.
2. Place test-taking on your agenda to discuss with his teacher. (Teacher-parent contacts are reviewed in the next chapter.)
3. Talk to your child. He may have something tangible to offer. Consider that his views, though honest, may not include all of the real reasons but are, nevertheless, worthwhile.

4. Look at tests sent home for hints as to what may be wrong.

Causes and Cures

There is a possibility that your child, the student:

- Never learned the content material sufficiently. Under typical conditions, students earn lower scores than they should because they haven't concentrated enough on the subject. The entire remedial program is based on shrinking this reason. Reexamine your efforts on implementing the program, especially the chapter on homework.
- Learned the subject only superficially and forgot important segments. He did not internalize an understanding of the subject so that it could be recalled as needed. As before, review the remedial program. If he can do his homework as outlined, he knows enough to do well on tests.
- Didn't review his assignments adequately or properly before the test. He missed some essential step. His notes were disorganized or incomplete. He concentrated on the wrong material. He tried to master too much with too little time. (The homework chapter is not long but vital in turning an underachiever around. Review it point by point until your child handles every aspect with ease.)
- Has an affective dissonance. This is my term for overinvolvement of emotions in a testing climate. As Adele found out, this was Wally's predicament. How does one attack an examination with all his cognitive resources if he's blinded by panic? The typical ''nail biters'' are, obviously, more nervous than they should be. Their lack of composure may be because they:
  - Have a fear of failing and all it entails.
  - Recoil from competitive endeavors.
  - Have been influenced by unpleasant test-taking experiences.

o Harbor feelings of inadequacy. (Review the prescriptive chapters on self-esteem and confidence-building.)

The prescriptive chapters provide procedures for countering each of the emotional liabilities enumerated.

- Has a subconscious urge to fail as a punishment for himself and/or others. This difficulty implies the possibility of a mental disorder and is beyond the scope of this writing. See a psychotherapist.
- Lacks the test-taking skills needed to present his knowledge and understanding of the subject. He may:

  o Not apportion and budget his time correctly during essay tests.
  o Write too much, get sidetracked, and omit essential facts.
  o Miss the point of a question and respond incorrectly.
  o Get confused in objective tests and search for hidden meanings which are not there.
  o Linger too long over questions in objective tests instead of completing the work on time.

Taking Tests

1. Redirect Skills
A test is a homework assignment in wolf's clothing. Why did Washington cross the Delaware? The student must now apply his homework know-how to somewhat different conditions about basically the same material.

The fundamentals of learning are unchanged. Learning, in addition to understanding, includes the ability to present the same material in different forms. During a test, the test paper becomes the new recipient of the child's knowledge.

The components of a subject are of little value unless they can be used. In learning to learn, the parent must stress the importance of applying knowledge to new situations.

2. Follow Directions
Teachers in school and even in colleges commonly write across a student's paper, "You missed the point" or "Good

answer, but not to the question I asked.'' Parents frequently complain, ''He knows the work but not while taking tests.'' Wrong. If he knew the work before, then he knew the work when taking the test. The problem is that he doesn't place the right answer in the right place.

The student who has developed good homework skills recognizes the purpose of the assignment and attempts to fulfill that purpose. The same student reading a test question recognizes the intent of the question and responds to it specifically rather than answering with related information. He listens as his mental voice reads the question. His listening skills help him understand the question posed. He doesn't answer something else.

He has only a limited time to complete several questions. If there are three questions in an essay-type examination, he shouldn't spend half his time on one question and only 25% each on the others. A few seconds of planning are in order.

What is the main theme of the question? Remember, he has already become proficient in making such judgments from his numerous homework assignments. What are the most important points that need to be included in his answer? He then plans his attack by focusing on just those elements without adding miscellaneous bits of information that cross his mind as he is writing. He stays with the main theme without adding the irrelevant material and without going off on tangents. He then quickly reads his answer to be sure it's developed as he intended and moves on to the next question using the same procedure. He writes about Washington's actions and why George took them. He doesn't mention the color of his uniform.

The same homework and listening skills will help him answer the short objective questions such as true-false, fill-ins, completions, and multiple-choice.

What is being asked?

What information pertains to this topic?

What information is most important?

What is the most likely correct answer?

He has also learned to use a variation of the economy of time again from doing homework. He knows how to focus on one question at a time and disregards unrelated thoughts. He reads, thinks, answers, and then attacks the next question.

3. Test Preparation

The time to start preparing for an examination is the day the subject is introduced in class. Few children will do this, but the underachieving child may have to make some special efforts. He should never allow himself to fall too far behind. You, as parent-teacher, have already provided a built-in regulator. His daily homework assignments, properly done, apportion the learning material into absorbable segments. The content of any topic should be on a continuum. Today's lesson becomes the foundation for tomorrow's. The two, together, provide the substructure for the third day's work, and so on. By keeping abreast with his homework, the learner is unconsciously preparing for the inevitable test.

When a test is announced, the child should start to review his notes and have notes to review. Cramming is a widespread affliction that should be avoided by the underachiever in particular. Last-minute studying can produce results on a test, but jamming it into a resisting mind leads to early extinction. The college student, taking an elective course in physical anthropology, may not care if he ever recalls the details of the *Australopithecus*; he just wants credit for the course. The elementary school student must build his future on the early school grades. He'll use his reading, computational, and writing skills all his life.

4. Test Practice

Every homework assignment is test preparation. The child learns to repeat the content material taught in the class, keep orderly notes, and utilize the built-in review mechanism. As he reexamines the material, the parent helps by creating a few questions. Doing "prep" tests does more than refresh the material for the youngster. It provides practice.

Give the child your own test at home and observe his test-taking techniques. When available, use the teacher's old test or one similar to it. Judge his ability to take tests. Does he have the required information and understanding he is being tested for? Can he put his thoughts on paper in some coherent fashion? Use an occasional essay-type question or three to four objective test questions on a given day.

Psychologists have recognized the *improvement that comes*

from repeated test-taking and refer to such experiences as becoming *test-wise*. People who take the same test or very similar ones tend to produce higher scores each time even though they have never seen the answers. Conversance with the format of a test and a degree of general test-taking skill produces desired results. Provide your child with as much practice as you can before an actual test.

Children need to overcome their tendency to include extraneous information in their answers. Practice should include identifying salient elements and excluding the rest. For instance, his geography homework may emphasize the United States. You may extract some items from homework assignments that you foresee will appear in tests as separate questions, or in combination for an essay question. First, have your child practice identifying the information that answers the question and nothing else.

Where is the United States?
The United States is:
A large country
One of the world's greatest democracies
South of Canada
In the western hemisphere
An English-speaking nation
In North America
A nation of many races and religions
Bordered by the Atlantic and Pacific oceans
North of Mexico
Home of the American people

If he omitted a statement that should be included, point it out. He might have just missed it or he might have thought it didn't belong. You now have to be the expert and explain why it does. If he included a statement that is not pertinent, have a discussion until he understands why.

Wally, as he began to overcome his excessive nervousness, was confronted with the above geography question. Since it was a subjective exam, he added the notation that Alaska did not fit into his responses nor did another state in the Pacific. When the test was returned, the teacher praised him for his astuteness but wanted to know why that other state in the Pacific wasn't identified.

"Can you name it?" she asked.

"Hawaii," he answered promptly.

"Why didn't you say that in the test?"

"I couldn't spell it."

The same information may be used to compose a few factual questions. Keep them simple. He's in elementary school.

The United States is in the _____ hemisphere.

Canada is south of the United States. True or False?

The United States is
   a. An island nation
   b. A great democracy
   c. In South America
   d. In Canada

Practice won't make him perfect but will make him better. It will help get him used to taking tests and make him review the subject matter each time you present him with a new question.

5. Check Yourself

Your remedial efforts, as delineated earlier, should obviate any necessity for special attention to test-taking. A bit of jitters may even be conducive to good performance but, if you suspect a serious test-taking weakness, review the program. Some areas may require reinforcement.

You should have:

1. Built his confidence by raising his level of self-esteem
2. Overcome his unreasonable fears of the unknown or challenges
3. Prepared him to face a learning or testing situation alone
4. Arranged for him to have experienced enough success to accept the possibility of occasional failure without undue concern
5. Integrated his skills into waste-reducing habits
6. Familiarized him with the process of making intelligent and immediate decisions, and selecting the best answer available from the given choices

7. Provided him with skill in answering the question asked, including the main theme, by using a brief outline concept. In his mind he arranges a few facts in sequence that will provide the answer sought
8. Increased his ability to focus his attention on the problem at hand
9. Enlarged his armamentarium of reserve techniques for problem solving based on his numerous homework experiences

Wrap-Up

Grades are directly related to test scores, but the test results may reflect the learner's test-taking abilities rather than his knowledge.

Many children and adults do not perform at their best while taking written examinations.

Some children and adults are extremely inept while taking a test due to emotional anxiety.

Professionals often overlook the evaluation of a child's test-taking ability as a possible cause of less than expected performance.

The ability to do well on tests may help or hamper a person throughout life.

Parents can play a significant role in helping children master test-taking techniques. As with many other abilities, the earlier they start, the better the results.

Test-taking utilizes many of the same procedures recommended for homework. Skills learned in home assignments are transferable to the testing arena.

Parents should evaluate the test-taking ability of an underachieving child to be sure of optimal performance. The suggestions for improving overall school work still supply.

Test preparation should be a routine for the child and not a cause for anxiety.

Children suffering from an inability to do well on tests may be helped by the remedial program which addresses the emotional side of the learning coin.

Familiarity with tests should help all children become test-wise.

19

Working with the School

The Wrong Question

"Why," Mrs. Bennett asked, "can't the schools do more for children like Josh? Why do they dismiss them as *just* under-achievers?" Her son, you may remember, was diagnosed as merely being a child who didn't do his best.

Parents by the hundreds of thousands ask similar questions each year and receive the obvious answers. The problem is that they're asking the wrong questions.

Underachievers, as a rule, do not disrupt classroom activity, especially in the elementary grades. They usually are not disciplinary problems. They are not emotionally unstable. In fact, they're displaying an adjustment that enables them to slide by in unfavorable circumstances. They're square pegs in round holes that pretend to fit. They're not similar to the mentally or sensory handicapped children who require specific programs. They do not belong in the catchall for children with neurological problems known as the learning-disabled. They're not disadvantaged by their environment. In fact, they come from all social-economic strata. They do not attract attention to themselves as individuals or special subsidies from the state or federal government.

Mrs. Bennett and the other parents in her position can complain to the state capitals and Washington, D.C. as frequently and as forcefully as desired but they will likely not produce any tangible results. The typical response is that "There's nothing wrong with your child. Just make him study harder." This answer is misleading, frequently not do-able and, sometimes, just wrong.

Josh Bennett represents millions of students who may, by my definition, be classified as underachievers. There are millions of other students who are not *significantly* below their potential in school performance but who are, nevertheless, not doing work near their optimal level. The two groups together account for the "rising tide of mediocrity" that characterizes the nation's educational system today. Few Americans still hold the position that schools are doing well. Current disagreements center on solutions to acknowledged problems. Since clear answers to a threatening situation are unavailable, people are supporting single-phrase remedies. "Back to basics," "Phonics," "Stay in school," "More money."

Politicians emphasize that they favor "good schools" and echo empty phrases such as "thorough and efficient." Legislators arrange for state control over some school districts, courts mandate changes, citizen groups replace elected school boards, districts are entrusted to universities, lay councils are formed, and revenue-raising and distribution procedures are altered. As a parent, your obligation is to ask the right questions.

The Right Question

"I'm told that the educational lag from the time that changes are approved until they are actually implemented is ten to twenty years," Mrs. Bennett says. "I have little confidence in the suggestions I've heard but even if they're effective, I can't wait that long. *How do I help Josh right now?*"

Mrs. Bennett, in her brief statement, is acutely accurate in her understanding and concern. Sociologists are familiar with the time required for new ideas, no matter how worthwhile, to permeate society. Though many people would like to believe differently, the field of education is not a leader in innovative curricula. A few programs, currently available to fill specific needs, are excellent. More are coming. The delay is caused by the nature of the educational structure and is not the subject of this work.

A day I remember in detail illustrates both the educational lag and the benefits of test preparation and practice as described in the last chapter. The year was 1969. The thermometer was high even for July as I roamed the halls of my university. On this day I had to face six professors from the Department of Psychology and a seventh from the Department of Education in a Star Chamber ordeal known as the "defense of the dissertation." This was the final hurdle in earning a doctorate and, sometimes, the end of a career. I knew many students who had completed the course work and passed their tests but were stymied by the dissertation. They were branded as ABDs—all but the dissertation.

I felt confident that I knew everything in my field anyone on the committee had a right to ask. I felt confident I knew more about the subject of my dissertation after four years of intensive study than anyone present. I had submitted two volumes describing my research and experimentation which I supported with very sophisticated statistics.

As I entered the examination room, I felt a slight twinge of apprehension which disappeared when the first question was asked.

This tale illustrates the necessity of preparation and practice advocated earlier. The principles remain the same at every level of the scholastic ladder. Your child should enter any test situation or interview knowing that he is ready. He'll still feel emotion and some element of uncertainty, but the odds will be on his side.

The other reason for relating this episode illustrates the educational lag. After I left the examination room while the "jury" considered its "verdict," I again roamed the halls and stopped at the office of Don Hammill. Dr. Hammill, a pioneer in the study of learning disabilities, had just completed a well-crafted and informative manuscript, which was published shortly thereafter, about learning disabilities. Twelve years later, I watched a television program in utter consternation as an interviewer spoke with the mother of a learning-disabled child. The interviewer, in an informative voice, explained to the audience that learning disability was a brand new field requiring new thinking and innovative teaching approaches. Many children, hitherto ignored, were going to be helped. New? Many thousands of educators, including myself, had done considerable work on the subject throughout the 1970s.

My discussion with Dr. Hammill ended when I was summoned to the examination room. The committee had completed its deliberations. I thought of words that I might yearn for in other situations: an umpire yelling "Safe!"; a foreman proclaiming "Not guilty"; a physician announcing "Benign." For the first time that day I recognized some nervous symptoms that were more than a twinge. Someone had lengthened the hallway to the examination room. Einstein was right. The clock slowed as my thought processes accelerated. Finally, I arrived. One of the professors stood, impassibly, leaning on the doorjamb and beckoned me with his finger. He seemed a bit too self-satisfied to please me. Sure. He had nothing to worry about.

As I approached, he said, "Come in, Doctor."

A Parental Plan

You should consider all your options to rectify your child's underachievement. If the public school can't do the job for your child, go find a school that can. Many private schools are quite good and one may be just the appropriate tonic for your child. If the cost for tuition and transportation is not prohibitive, you should investigate and weigh the possibilities of this alternative carefully. Private schools should not be considered for temporary placement. If the private sector is your best choice, prepare for the long-term. Taking a child out of public school, placing him into a different educational milieu and then returning him to where the trouble developed may be counterproductive.

Tutoring centers across the land advertise extensively. They are designed to supplement the program of whatever school your child already attends. These "centers," usually profit-making organizations, are competitive with each other and vie for your dollar. Their best advertisements are satisfied parents who will tell others about the program.

Tutoring organizations generally use instructional materials available to the public schools as well as the same teaching procedures. Their advantage lies in the individualized and small group attention they're prepared to offer.

You must decide on the best course for your child and, to do so, you need to ask some important questions:

- The centers focus on children who fail or are close to it. Do they offer a program that will help *your* child? If your child is a youngster with "A" potential but with "C" grades, what kind of program do they have for him?

- As with most businesses, the centers generally imply a high success rate. Testimonials to support this contention are not enough. The investment you must make is quite large. What results will they guarantee?

- If they offer some assurance of success, is this in the form of additional tutoring without charge or will they return fees you have paid? You could reasonably allow them several hundred dollars as a "deductible" on their gross charges, but what are they willing to do beyond that?

- What are their fees? You want all costs itemized before providing even the smallest deposit. Even if they offer some kind of incentive plan or discount, expect to pay a considerable amount. Their hourly rate will punch holes into your budget but, from their perspective, is not excessive. They use current materials and equipment, have all of the usual business overhead, may pay a franchise fee, and must produce a profit to stay open.

- Are you convinced that a learning center will be able to (1) raise your child's performance level (especially in reading and mathematics); and (2) diagnose and remediate the source of his problem? Symptomatic relief, as in medicine, is only temporary. You must excise the cause.

- If tutoring in the academic areas is required to raise your child's academic level while you also provide remedial measures at home, then consider a tutor not affiliated with a commercial center. Many teachers, at reasonable rates, provide such services in their own homes or yours.

The Right Question

The best practical alternative for the majority of parents is to keep their child in the same public school he now attends but with a parental intervention strategy. This scheme should include provisions to cooperate with the school and a system for the school to reciprocate. Three parties will benefit and there will be no losers. The school gets the credit and support it needs while raising its standing, you have no additional costs, and your child's level of work rises. Before starting the help-the-school-help-your-child-program, you should recognize some realities about schools that are not generally understood by critics.

- Schools cannot decrease class size or add additional teacher aides or special services without increasing their spending.
- Schools are designed to serve whole communities and cannot individualize every program for every child, all day, every day.
- Schools cannot return to the "good old days" if they ever even existed. They function in today's world with current problems and limitations.
- Schools are only a part of society and not responsible for all societal ills. They did not create the drug scene, latchkey children, or current social turmoil.
- Teachers and administrators can and are willing to help your child, especially if you will render some assistance. Educators yearn for cooperative parents. Consider yourself part of the teaching team. Teachers will take care of the academic subjects if you will help make learning possible.
- Don't underestimate the competency and willingness of the vast majority of today's elementary school teachers. The ineffectual performance by the schools as a whole is due to whirlwind social changes, revised societal outlooks, needs, and expectations, as well as revolution-

ary technological developments. In this climate leaders have remained moribund and politicians have levied catch phrases instead of taxes.

Teacher Contacts

You must *overcome any reluctance* to confer with officials of the school to resolve any issue dealing with your child. If you feel anxious about approaching school people because you lack an equivalent background or know little about education, remember that community goodwill is absolutely essential for school people. They survive on public monies. Their need for materials, equipment, buildings, and salary increases is ongoing. Once having made the contact, the experience will serve as a base for future conferences which become easier and then routine.

Some suggestions:

- Be on time. A teacher has a tight schedule all day. Evening meetings, though necessary, are a burden.
- Wait your turn. Other parents are interested in their children's progress, too.
- Leave your ego at home. You are not there to impress the teacher with anything about yourself, except your desire to help and cooperate. You are there to solve a problem, check on your child's progress, evaluate a placement, or gain some insight into the school's activities.
- Start the discussion as if you understand this is to be the beginning of a collaborative effort. You will find that a confrontation is unnecessary in virtually every case. The teacher and you have a common goal. You're both seeking favorable results. Simply put, she is on your side. Keep her there.
- The initial meeting should *set the tone* for the future. Treat educators as the intelligent adults they are and expect the same treatment in return. Do not prolong small talk. Get to the point of the meeting. Although you should not monopolize the teacher's time, you do want to see the entire picture.

- Ask questions. Initially, the teacher is likely to tell you
  nice things about your child that you want to hear.
  Unless your child is a trouble-maker, she'll limit any
  learning problems to one or two areas. You enjoy
  hearing praise about your child but you're there because
  your offspring is not progressing properly. Get down to
  business. You want this to be the meeting that launches
  a home and school effort to improve the performance of
  your child. Ask the questions that will shed light on
  what he's doing at school. Ask about the course of
  study, the materials, the equipment, the teacher support
  systems (aides, specialists, supervisors, counselors,
  reading teachers, psychologists).

    Ask about *your* child.

    What is his behavior like in class?

    Does he participate in class activities?

    How does his attention span compare with other
      children?

    Does he show more interest in some subjects?

    Does he lose interest in any particular topic?

    Is his work getting better, worse, or is he on a
      plateau?

    What skills does the teacher think he needs to
      improve?

    What is her advice?

    What does she think you, as a parent, can contribute?

- If you are requested to make a determination about your
  child, such as a special placement, delay your response.
  Do not make important decisions immediately. Explain
  that you want to consider the matter. Take the information home with you. Discuss it with another adult who
  is interested in the welfare of your child. If possible,
  discuss it with your child. Evaluate all of the alternatives before making a final decision. Perhaps you will
  have some new questions or need other information.
  Make an appointment for another conference.

- If you are satisfied that you have all of the necessary
  data about your child's progress, end the meeting with
  an *acknowledgment of your feelings*. The teacher is
  entitled to a word of appreciation for her help which

may offset some unjustified criticism from another source.

Eyes on the Doughnut

Your role as a parent is not to usurp the teacher's position but to make it possible for the instructor to teach your child successfully. You are, of course, free to render some assistance in subject matter to help your child overcome a specific obstacle. You may add pieces of information or correct misconceptions but you shouldn't undertake to teach the entire subject. You, at times, can be a spot remover; the teacher is the professional dry cleaner.

You have enough work to do in terms of sharing your values, teaching your child how to learn better, building his self-esteem and providing general guidance. You already have a good picture of your child at home and at play and now you have added the important view of the teacher.

By this time, whether two minutes or ten have elapsed, you have an impression of the teacher and, just as important, she has formed one about you. Your signals should say that you are a very busy but very interested parent and you intend to work with the school. You expect the school to cooperate with you. If the teacher starts to terminate the meeting, hang in for a few seconds more. You first want to open the lines of further communication with her. Since continuous meetings are not practical, is there a time when the two of you should converse by telephone? Are letters or phone calls acceptable? Can numbers and addresses be exchanged?

The communication between the two of you could be carried on through your child or through the mail. Neither of you needs to bother with a lengthy exposition. The teacher may write a sentence or two on homework assignments being returned and on graded tests. Sometimes just a phrase or word will be enough. Though brief, these observations can be very helpful to you.

"Notice that he didn't follow directions."
"He misunderstood the question."

"He spent too much time on the first part and then couldn't finish."

"He didn't think the assignment through before beginning."

"He wasn't prepared."

"He seemed to know the material but couldn't express himself."

"His scribbling indicates he rushed through the work."

These teacher comments point to weaknesses that can be corrected, and are therefore of considerable value. This is the kind of communication you want to establish with the teacher.

Poor work or good work will present its own picture. You want the teacher to be attuned to his shortcomings so that corrective actions may be taken. If at times you find the teacher's notations unhelpful, return the paper with a question of your own.

"Just what did he lack in order to answer the questions properly? What areas must we work on?"

If you don't get a timely or adequate response, add a line to your next communication. "I'll call you." And do.

The variety of helpful observations by a teacher are endless. An experienced, capable instructor will note errors and omissions and suggest alternative approaches. Teachers see what the child does wrong. Parents can remediate.

A "Mrs. Bennett," a parent, can sometimes read a recommendation coming from the teacher at school and respond with "I don't know how to do that."

A "Mrs. Leady," a teacher, can then respond with suggestions. The teacher and the parent, pulling simultaneously in the same direction, can increase Josh's skills. A coordinated effort doesn't just double the possibilities of improvement but increases the chances geometrically.

Wrap-Up

The remedial program requires you to involve yourself in the development of your youngster. That is an appropriate role for a parent. In addition, you must utilize the services of your school district and help the school help your child. Your duty as a citizen is related to the long-term improvement of schools. That may happen eventually. But your concern as a parent is immediate.

An isolated underachiever does not attract the attention of the school system. You must bring your individual concerns to the attention of your child's teacher.

The educational time lag is horrendous. Improved programs take one-half of forever before being instituted. Therefore, parents must work with the school as it exists.

An ongoing communication system established between parent and teacher tends to be a highly effective and practical solution to the problems of the underachiever.

20

Reading
Home Style

MOTHER: I talked to the reading teacher, but now I'm more confused than ever.

EDUCATIONAL THERAPIST: You probably weren't listening.

MOTHER: Do you always take the teacher's side?

THERAPIST: Only when she's right.

MOTHER: How often is that?

THERAPIST: Most of the time. This is costing you money. Why don't you get to the problem.

MOTHER: You know the problem. Chris is a poor reader. So anyway, I talked to the specialist and I took notes. They're here somewhere. Here. Listen to this.

THERAPIST: Just summarize what she said in your own words, please.

MOTHER: I can't. She said a lot about reading deficits being caused by visual perceptual problems and configurational confusion.

THERAPIST: You don't have to review the list.

MOTHER: No. No. That's why I'm perplexed. I don't know what all this means. Auditory blending. Auditory, visual discrimination. And listen to this. Integrational capacities. Dominance.

THERAPIST: I get the picture.

MOTHER: You're not taping this, are you?

THERAPIST: Yes. There's the recorder.

MOTHER: I don't want anything I say made public.

THERAPIST: It won't be.

MOTHER: Never? Promise?

THERAPIST: I learn from listening to the tapes of these sessions. If I ever use the dialogue, no one will be identified. No one will listen to the tape.

MOTHER: All right. There's more. Directional confusion. Spatial disorientation.

THERAPIST: You don't have to . . .

MOTHER: Wait a minute. How about visual motor, perceptual motor, and motor coordination? How many motors does Chris have?

THERAPIST: Let me see the list. Thanks. There's some overlap and duplication here. She didn't read you these points, did she?

MOTHER: No. She said something like "involved complexities" and I said something like "lousy teaching."

THERAPIST: She was just trying to say that simple explanations aren't always the answer.

MOTHER: But how can I deal with this stuff?

THERAPIST: You can't. That's why the schools should do the formal teaching.

MOTHER: Then I'm supposed to sit back and do nothing?

THERAPIST: Of course not. Teach reading.

MOTHER: You just contradicted yourself.

THERAPIST: Not really. It's a matter of definition. Parents should supplement the program of the school. Teach reading—home style.

MOTHER: Explain.

THERAPIST: Make it informal. It's not a subject. It's a tool. You can't do much without it.

MOTHER: I see. Tell Chris he can't be what he wants to be unless he can read. Reading is vital.

THERAPIST: Tell him no such thing. Let him discover the value of reading himself.

MOTHER: How?

THERAPIST: By the reality. It's like an old-fashioned automobile mechanic. He grew up watching his father or others dismantle motors, but they needed tools—the right tools. There are jobs pliers can do, but sometimes a wrench can do it better. The mechanic learns that having the right tool for the job makes it easier and faster. Then he learns that quality tools are better than cheap ones. You could have told him all of that but he's really impressed when he discovers it himself.

MOTHER: I'm not so sure I follow. Reading is like a tool?

THERAPIST: Reading is a tool. It's even called a tool subject. It's used in almost every content subject there is. Without reading, ninety percent of effectiveness in school is lost. Maybe more.

MOTHER: So how should I start?

THERAPIST: Make Chris read. Not in a prescribed manner or at a set time. That's for school. Make him read to do other things. Convert your household into a reading laboratory.

MOTHER: You mean no television?

THERAPIST: Television is fine. But everything can't revolve around watching TV all the time. Create some other activities.

MOTHER: Like what?

THERAPIST: There's no limit to the possibilities. I'll start and you'll get the idea. Write notes to Chris. Put them on a home-sized chalkboard or on paper or on a message board. Start with simple things like:

"I'll be home at six."

"Set the table."

"There are cookies in the jar."

"Use the big glass for your milk."

MOTHER: Should I get a list of words from school for his grade?

THERAPIST: No. Use everyday language. There's no such thing as an "order of learning" vocabulary. He'll learn words as he needs them.

Make him take phone messages in writing. If he can't write well enough, start with a prepared sheet like the printed ones that say, "While you were away." Have him put in the time the person phoned, the name of the person, and the phone number. He can ask the caller how to spell his name. As soon as he can, have him include a message such as "Repairman will call." It doesn't matter if he misspells. He'll improve.

MOTHER: So I should teach him how to write properly?

THERAPIST: Don't separate reading and writing. Chris can improve both skills simultaneously. Involve him in all obvious reading possibilities.

MOTHER: I'm afraid they're not so obvious to me.

THERAPIST: Books, Magazines. Labels. Signs. Menus. Cards. Letters. Television captions. Wherever he goes, there are things to read. Have him do it.

MOTHER: Buy books too?

THERAPIST: You can, but use the libraries—the most underrated and underpublicized institution we have. They have more than books. Look at their tapes. Use all the modern information storage technology for public use. There's so much available to occupy children besides television. Give Chris the opportunity to become thoroughly familiar with libraries.

MOTHER: Anything else?

THERAPIST: There's no limit. Reading is like the one nut or the first potato chip. Once he's had that first taste he'll go back for more. He'll find stories that interest him and articles that provide the information he wants. He'll discover practical value in reading, like how to assemble toys or make ice cream. His curiosity will be satisfied by reading.

MOTHER: Should I pick the subject matter?

THERAPIST: You can make suggestions but don't lock him in. Do what Edison's parents did. Make his curriculum the world.

   Chris can read about anything he finds interesting as long as you find it acceptable. Dinosaurs. Sports. Toys. Cars. Space. It's a big universe.

MOTHER: And I should coordinate it with his school studies.

THERAPIST: No.

MOTHER: No?

THERAPIST: You're not a miniature school. You have no set course of study. If he wants to read about a school topic, that's fine. If he must read about a school topic because it's part of his homework, that's all right. Otherwise, let him choose topics of interest to him. Or just let him explore some door you've opened for him.

MOTHER: Wait a second. I need another pen. All right, go on.

THERAPIST: It's not a circumscribed program. In fact, it's not a program at all. It's a way of life. Follow that pattern. Books make good gifts. Give him some. Suggest that he give them to others. Let him look at the shelves in a store and examine books. Help him make selections.

   Have him create a personal library of books and magazines. He can even lend them to relatives and friends and keep records.

One of the best methods to use is example. He'll be influenced by what others do in his home. You might try having reading periods. This can be set periods in the evening such as before bed or on weekends. You may have a silent reading time with each member reading his own material or have someone read aloud, or both.

MOTHER: When do I do all this? I work, you know.

THERAPIST: Reading time can be fifteen minutes. The other techniques are interwoven with daily activities. You plan little but you take advantage of every reading opportunity. Much of your effort will depend on your attitude. It's great fun to read. Communicate that feeling to your son.

MOTHER: If I don't tie home reading with school reading, how do I know where to begin? Suppose he can't read what I give him or what he chooses?

THERAPIST: Start with the short notes you know he can read. Then help him as he moves up to more difficult passages.

MOTHER: Should I teach him phonics to sound out words?

THERAPIST: There's an ongoing controversy about that; phonics versus the look-say method, the system of learning to recognize whole words at a glance.

MOTHER: Which side do you favor?

THERAPIST: Both. Children learn to read by remembering a word after they've used it. Phonics is a good support system that helps sometimes. It's particularly useful at the beginning of reading when you can use families of words, words that rhyme. If he becomes familiar with "mat" and knows the sound of "b," he can read "bat." The same applies to cat, rat, fat, hat, vat, pat, and sat.

MOTHER: What approach should I take?

THERAPIST: Anything and everything. Let the school use sequences, skill components, objectives, and everything they think will work. But, if your child is a poor reader, then obviously their methods aren't doing too well.

MOTHER: Like in my son's case.

THERAPIST: Yes, but that doesn't make them wrong. You can provide the missing piece; that is, take into account your kid's individuality. There are more than five billion people in the world. Not a single one of them is another Chris.

MOTHER: You mean that I should provide whatever the school doesn't?

THERAPIST: Right again. You know his interests and that is the greatest motivator. Also, equally important, is that by applying the remedial program you become familiar with his learning style. You now have two weapons in your helping arsenal that the teacher doesn't have: You know his personal way of learning and his major interests. Use them.

MOTHER: Hold on a minute. You're telling me that I shouldn't worry about such things as his reading books, workbooks, or following special learning systems. Instead, I should just open the doors to all kinds of reading experiences—outside of school? Do I test him?

THERAPIST: No, he'll be evaluated in the classroom.

MOTHER: I still have questions. What do I do if he's reading and finds that he doesn't know a certain word?

THERAPIST: Tell him the word; both how to pronounce it and what it means. Don't make a big thing of it. If the situation allows, go back afterwards and review the words he didn't know. See if he remembers them. Can he use them in a sentence? If he's forgotten some, and he will, tell him again.

MOTHER: What about that controversy? Shouldn't he try to sound it out?

THERAPIST: If he can apply "instant" phonics, all right. If he can sound out the word quickly, that's fine. If he has to work out each syllable with difficulty, he's going to break the rhythm of his reading.

MOTHER: Which means?

THERAPIST: He'll forget what he was reading and he'll miss the message.

MOTHER: Reading comprehension.

THERAPIST: Right. Besides, stopping too often makes reading stilted and frustrating. If you want to see a child in agony, watch him trying to decode a word that doesn't come out. Then another and another. That kind of reading isn't fun. It's one of the big turnoffs.

MOTHER: What do you mean "doesn't come out"?

THERAPIST: Phonics only works with some words. Others do not lend themselves to phonics.

MOTHER: Give me an example.

THERAPIST: L-E-A-D. Is that pronounced "leed" or "led"? You have to go by the context, how a word is used in a sentence. There are so many ways to pronounce some letters. If the child has to guess, he's in trouble. There are over one hundred-fifty rules in phonics. Readers know them from experience, not direct study. Of course, some people would argue with me.

MOTHER: You're saying I shouldn't help him pronounce a word?

THERAPIST: No, not exactly. Just don't rely on phonics. It's helpful, especially for simple words. But reading is learned like speaking. Sounds are associated with meaning. In reading the sound is associated with the configuration of the word and the meaning naturally follows. Your best bet is to use what works for Chris.

MOTHER: It's getting complicated. I think I'll just ignore theory and provide many, many reading opportunities. I'll give him lots of practice.

THERAPIST: Now you've got it.

The Solution is Simple (According to Some People)

The state senator, never known as an erudite speaker, nevertheless traveled from county to county addressing any group that would invite him.

Whenever his party won a majority of seats in the senate, he became chairman of the educational committee. His background was in small business, but he continually expressed an interest in improving schools. Now, he seemed especially inspired. He had a cause—phonics. If phonics were reinstituted, Johnny would learn to read.

One day, the senator concluded his presentation to a group of elementary school principals of a city school district. "Questions?" he asked confidently.

"Are we going to get an increased state subsidy for next year?" a concerned administrator asked.

"Well, you know, I don't like to make predictions. I'll guarantee, however, that my committee will study the matter thoroughly. Any other questions? Please keep to the subject. Yes?"

"What are the chances of getting funds for a long-term study of phonics and other teaching techniques?"

The school superintendent, sitting next to the speaker, glared at the interrogator. The audience had been warned not to offend the senator. "We need this guy. He's got the power. Don't back him into a corner. He's not as mild as he appears."

"I believe you'll find," the senator responded, "that many studies have already been conducted. If you have an outstanding proposal, send it to Washington, not the state capital. We certainly don't want to waste funds on useless duplications. Next."

"Sir, how does phonics affect the child's comprehension of the material he's reading?"

"Well, he's not going to understand anything if he can't read the words in the first place," came the brusque reply.

"Senator, our school district has never stopped using phonics, but we're no more successful than anyone else in the state. Is there evidence to the contrary?"

"Well, it depends on what you mean by evidence. Anyhow, I'm running late so I'll have to break off now."

The senator seemed surprised as the audience stood and applauded enthusiastically. He smiled, waved, and headed for the door. The superintendent of schools scowled at some of the now discomforted principals.

The senator returned the following year to address the same group. His topic, the advance notice advised, was critical. "The necessity of putting geography back into the curriculum."

Home Systems

Sometimes the highly sophisticated reading instructional systems used by schools may not help your child learn to read at his appropriate level. The most effective approach for the parent is to make reading an integral part of the child's daily activities. Schools can compartmentalize reading. You shouldn't.

To keep your child motivated, reading should:

- Be fun
- Make sense to him
- Serve a useful purpose or just be interesting
- Be its own reward

Chris became a junior journalist. He listened to the news on the radio after school and prepared a report for the family. After dinner, he stood and delivered a summary of the day's news to an appreciative audience. His notes consisted of one-word reminders and a few short sentences. Weeks later, he graduated to gathering news items from the newspaper and combined them with the radio reports. Later still, he watched the television news as a critic. Chris combined his listening, writing, speaking, reading, and thinking skills for his one-minute headline announcements.

"Hey, Mom. How come there are two 'ch's' in church and neither sounds like the 'ch' in my name?"

Wrap-Up

The school bears the responsibility to teach, test and report on your child's progress. Your responsibility is to augment the program of the school. The combined effort should result in a good educational performance by your child.

Your parental responsibilities include: (1) strengthening the youngster's emotional side of learning; and (2) providing him with the cognitive attack skills that enable him to read.

The content of his studies is within the province of the school district, but if your child's reading ability is not at an acceptable level, you should employ your own, homemade reading program. Irrespective of any claims of other findings, the most effective plan to teach reading is practice. The more he reads, the better he will read.

Reading means comprehension. Saying words correctly, even with expression, is hardly helpful unless the child understands the meaning of the words. He should be able to explain the message in words of his own.

The reading specialist may enumerate many problems related to reading failure but most of these tend to disappear with growth. However, a poor attitude toward or a fear of reading may persist if not dealt with immediately.

The look-say versus phonics disagreement is overblown. Use anything that gets results for your child. Good teachers do just that.

The many dimensions of the mind are not fully understood.

Once that mental computer realizes that decoding of inscribed symbols is possible, a learning mechanism is set in motion. You have been, or should have been, reading to him from his earliest memories. He wants to start learning to do it himself just as soon as he can. Reading vocabularies are measured in the tens of thousands of words. These are hardly accumulated from direct, one-at-a-time study. Something else, an x-factor is at work.

Learning to read and other skills, including writing and arithmetic, require the same essentials as do all other challenges. The child must have his curiosity aroused in order to be motivated. Once motivated, the child continues in his pursuit as he receives intrinsic and extrinsic rewards along the way. Parents can enhance this process by creating ample opportunities outside the school.

21

On Being Different

The box squeaked as the voice announced, "Mr. Green is here."

Stan Brown and Jerome Green hadn't seen each other or communicated since high school. Stan, now a corporate president, was surprised to learn that Jerome worked for the company as a warehouse clerk. When an administrative position opened, Jerome applied for the job.

"Send him in. And Liz, please get someone to fix this intercom. Better yet, just replace it." Stan started toward the door when he heard a gentle knock.

"Who's that rapping at my chamber door?" he questioned facetiously.

"'Tis only me and nothing more," said the beaming Jerome as he entered, hand extended.

Stan ignored the hand and embraced his boyhood chum. Jerome's grin suggested the Cheshire cat; Stan struggled to suppress his emotion. The code is clear on that subject. Men don't cry.

"Sit over there near the coffee. Let me close this door. How the hell are you, Jerome?"

"I'm fine and now I'm Jerry."

"Jerry, huh? Momentous decision."

"We've moved closer to a unisex society."

"And you're older."

The squeaky box interrupted them.

"Yes, Liz."

"Maintenance says they'll be over first thing in the morning with a new intercom setup."

"Tell Mr. Maintenance that I'm leaving for lunch at noon. When I return, the job is to be complete and working."

"Showing them who's boss?" Jerome said, looking at the carpeting.

"No. Well. Maybe. Things are loose around here. Giving advice . . . Jerry?"

"You always considered it carefully before."

"Yes, I guess so. You and my mother were my mentors."

"Now you're at the top of the heap."

"No. This is a way station."

"What do you want to be? You're already president."

"Of a corporation."

Jerome's eyes twinkled. "I see."

"Let's get to you. I haven't heard anything since you dropped out of college."

"I was thrown out."

"Why?"

"For cheating on a test."

"Did you?"

"No."

Stan felt no need to wait for an explanation. "Then what?"

"Army."

"I won't ask. Since then . . . ?"

"Different jobs. Got married. Kids. Needed work so I came to this company." Jerome turned the conversation back to the college and army experiences before resuming his history.

"Then I heard you or someone with a name like yours was taking over so I thought I might apply for an administrative job."

"Getting ambitious?"

"I could use the money."

"Why the 'data recorders'?"

"I wanted to be sure it was you."

"Jerry. You're in no way qualified for the job. You can't have it. It's early, but let's go to lunch anyway."

For two hours the childhood friends reminisced about the great days of the past.

"Were they really that good?" asked Stan.

"No. Neither one of us fit in and school was boring. The only friends we had were each other and I had trouble at home. I didn't fit in there either. You, at least, had a great guidance counselor. Your mother."

"Still have. She's very much alive and active."

"And proud of her son, the president," added Jerome.

Stan said nothing, just stared. Then both, in unison, emphasized "—of a corporation."

"Are you really considering politics? That's not you. What are you going to do? Run for governor or the senate?" He then added, "To get into a good position."

"No. No intermediate stops. I'd like to go from industry to the White House."

"How are you going to do that?"

"I don't know. That's your job, the new one."

The two men returned from lunch as workmen were leaving Stan's office. He checked the new intercom. "Liz, please send a thank-you note to everyone involved in getting this contraption installed. You certainly sound better. And hold any calls not absolutely urgent."

The corporate president turned to the clerk.

"Jerry, what do you think?"

"I think I can't work for you."

"Why not?"

"I'm smarter than you are."

"So what? You're smarter than most everyone."

"I have trouble taking orders. I need reasons for everything. I break any work rule that gets in my way. I say what I think even if it offends people. I'm just different. So are you. I don't know how you do it."

Stan looked at Jerome's eyes. His brilliant schoolmate wasn't complaining; he was just stating facts. Jerome hadn't learned to be an achiever.

"Your word 'different' is apropos. You're right. I never really thought about it in those terms initially. I just worked out some ways of doing things that were good for me. I'm not sure, but I think it started when I was just a kid. I learned something early in dealing with people, thanks to my mother. It took years before enough of the pieces were in place to do me some good. And I'm still learning.''

An Incident Remembered

Stan, just approaching his sixth birthday, grappled with his mother's decision. She'd refused him permission to go shopping. It was "raining too hard." His initial reaction was vehement protest with some gesticulation and forced crying. He was about to, as in the past, resort to sulking about his plight when a thought restrained him.

He curled up in his favorite lounge chair where he could witness the cascade falling from the heavens. Remembering his mother's words, "cats and dogs," he thought, ridiculous. Pets don't fall from the sky. He could make an issue out of that. No, he reflected. It wouldn't work. There was something else. What was he trying to recall? Something had happened that he could use for changing his mother's mind.

Safety? He didn't have to cross a street to get to the store. No. She knew that.

Maybe he could ask her again with a chain of "Pleases." Yes. And if that didn't work, he could be bad. What did she call it? Throw a tantrum or something like that.

No. Those things weren't any good. He would be punished.

There must be a better . . . Wait a minute. The memory of an incident lit up a cerebral compartment. It was a long time ago. Maybe last month. Mom and Dad argued over buying a new washing machine. Dad said no, just as Mom did now. But then Mom pulled out all the repair bills on the old washer and showed them to Dad. "What'll we do, fix it again?" she asked. Dad inspected the stack and gave in. He did! Mom convinced him she was right.

Armed with an innovative strategy, Stan approached his

mother again. Looking at the shower of rain through the window, she again said no, but perhaps a little later.

Stan was ready.

"Mom, do I have a raincoat?"

"Yes, dear."

"Does it have a hood to go over my head?"

His mother became a bit wary. "You know it does."

"Do I have rubbers for my shoes? And an umbrella?"

"Yes."

With his hands on his hips, Stan paused for effect.

"Why?"

On his journey to the store, Stan felt the incomparable uplift of spirit that accompanies success. Imprinted on his mind was the lesson he had learned. Sometimes you can win without shouting or crying or sulking. Sometimes obstacles can be overcome with reason.

Achievement following defeat can be intoxicating. You can deal with people if you use the right method.

Different Folks

"The greatest teacher," opined Stan, "is experience."

"Not exactly an original thought," Jerome interjected.

"I don't know if it's possible to have an original thought," countered Stan.

"Now we are philosophizing."

"I'll just ignore you," Stan said pleasantly.

"People are different from each other. Sometimes, the dissimilarity goes to an extreme and separates a person from the group."

"We're separatists," Jerry added. "Too damn smart."

"No, you're a separatist," Stan clarified. "I've learned to live with and use my intellect. That's what anyone with any physical, mental, cultural, or ethnic disparity should do."

"Sounds intriguing. Give me an example."

"Remember Mr. Garyel in junior high?"

"Sure."

"Remember how he had the first period free but had to

cover our class many times because Mrs. Locker was late?''

"Yes. He was so angry he couldn't suppress it. He always had another story about irresponsible people but we knew he meant Locker.''

"I don't think she could help it. People like her always had an excuse for being late. They irritated others and hurt themselves.''

"Stan, what's the point?''

"Learning how to deal with your own differences. Mrs. Locker could neither overcome her proclivity for being late, nor find a position where lateness didn't matter too much. Paul Watson did.''

"Oh, Paul. Clever guy. Yes, he was always late in school. What's his story?''

"Paul was consistently late for work, too. He never changed. He couldn't change. He became an electrical engineer and landed a job with a big firm. They liked his work but wouldn't tolerate his tardiness. Something about 'no special privileges' and 'bad examples.' They let him go. Paul got another job but the same thing happened. He then made the big adjustment. He started his own company and did subcontract work for others.''

"And?''

"He's on his way to being rich.

"Jerry, you want something. You say you need the money now. I know you need the satisfaction. You've got a gift and you're wasting it. But just being different isn't necessarily a blessing. You have to find a niche for yourself to take advantage of what you have.''

"If you're left-handed,'' observed his friend, "you can't play second, short, or third very well, but you have an advantage at bat.''

"Exactly. Find something suitable for yourself. If you're a natural night person, you're valuable if you want to work at night. Most people don't. If you are uncomfortable working inside a building, prepare for a job that's outside.''

"And if you're exceptionally brainy, become a corporate president,'' Jerome said, smiling again.

"It's the 'becoming' that has to be mastered. We

became friends because I challenged a teacher. It should have been a simple question. Since then, I learned to make my point by using other methods. I've had many learning experiences and I'll continue to have more.''

The Positive Negative Experience

Stan knew immediately that he had erred. The nine A.M. meeting of executives had started promptly and in just seven minutes he had applied a sharp blade to his throat. He imagined a red flow trickling down over his collar and ruining not only his shirt but his career. He remembered his boss's lecture.

"I don't want yes-men surrounding me. I want people with good ideas, great ideas. Understand?''

Stan waited silently, expectantly. He thought the question was rhetorical but quickly realized the boss wanted an affirmative. The subordinate supplied it with a vertical head movement.

"Now, whenever you get such a thought, present it. Immediately. Put it on the table for examination. In two minutes, it could lose its impact. They tell me you've got the smarts. Well, use them. Understand?''

"Yes, sir,'' Stan responded.

He remembered that bit of advice as well as the balance of his boss's welcoming words. For two years he had worked for this promotion and he intended to be successful in his new role. "Present it,'' his superior had emphasized. Now, following the advice given, Stan interrupted the VIP to present his idea to the group.

For seven minutes he reviewed the cost-effectiveness of the magazine advertisements of the past quarter. Stan clearly noted his dissatisfaction. "Television would work but we're not ready for that kind of expenditure. We need an alternative. I have a suggestion.''

The blade was selecting a site for its incision. "Radio,'' he stated emphatically. "I could work that written material into a good commercial for . . .'' Stan stopped. The room was too quiet. The other administrators weren't listening to him but were watching the chief executive.

Two eyes bulged from the boss's head beneath a furrow on his forehead. Stan understood. Faux pas. Present it immediately, but not when the almighty was speaking.

His leader had painted a picture of the person he thought he was, not his true self. Stan learned quickly, but perhaps not quickly enough. The room was no longer noiseless. The boss was playing a tune by alternately tapping his index and middle fingers of his left hand on the table.

Best Side Up

"You did the right thing," Jerome stated. "There's a principle involved. He told you to press forward with your thoughts when you had them. That's what you did. I would have done the same thing."

"Yes, you would have, but that's where our thinking has parted.

"His obstinacy would have clashed with yours and he would have won. I backed off."

"To run away and live to fight another day?"

"Something like that. I realized that this man, my chief, threw pat phrases around but didn't take them literally for himself. He was in charge. I wasn't.

"On reflection, I also realized I had been rude. You might have an idea, you might disagree, but you give people a chance to express their views."

"Especially if it's your boss," Jerome added. "And you learned that bit of 'courtesy' right then."

"No, actually I learned it in school. I just forgot it or ignored it. Both as a kid and a grownup, you have to work with authority figures. To work well, you have to have some understanding of how they operate."

"Even teachers?"

"Teachers are authority figures. You have to learn to 'read' people."

"Hooray for Freud!"

"No. I don't mean psychoanalysis. You should try to understand how they think, what they like, what is important to them. I reached a point where I was able to anticipate test questions.''

''You probably studied everything anyway, Stan.''

''No. A student can't study everything, especially in an advanced college class. The instructor assigns a book as a basic text and then gives you a reading list of thirty books. I never read more than three or four. I'm a good reader with a good memory but after awhile, I have trouble remembering who said what. I know, Jerry. You can remember every line.''

''Sure. But that got me tossed out of college.''

''Your stubbornness got you thrown out. You could have proven your ability and you had no right to attack your professor.''

''That's where we differ. I have to defend my principles.''

''So do I. But if the principle was *that* important to you then you could have set your sights on becoming a college president. With that position and some books and articles you could have worked for any teaching improvements you desired. You didn't change anything for the better by being expelled.''

''You should have been a preacher, Stan. How about those two army experiences I told. Laughing in formation and challenging the MPs?''

''How did you expect the battalion to take roll call? Have a thousand soldiers milling around and answering 'Here' to their names? Besides, they have to maintain discipline. If an officer gives an order in combat, he can't have a Jerome-type say, 'I think not.' ''

''What about those army cops driving the wrong way on a one-way road? A case of arrogance, right?''

''Perhaps. I don't know the circumstances. Maybe they were looking for someone or were answering a call by the shortest route. You didn't have the facts either. You had no right to judge. You should have gotten out of their way. Sometimes your 'principles' have to be set aside.''

''I hope, Stan, you don't take that approach to an extreme.''

''No. Of course not. If I were a cop and some sergeant told me to shoot a prisoner, I wouldn't do it. But I

wouldn't laugh at an army formation or take on the
military police, either.''

"But I'm different."

"Yes, but that's what different people must learn. They
have to adjust to society, reduce the effects of their
liabilities and . . .''

"I know. Employ their strengths where they can attain
optimal results.''

Living with Differences

An outside force may impinge on a child and disrupt the
sequential steps of his learning pattern. These may come in the
guise of negative experiences. They can take varied forms and
shapes. Parental intervention, such as the remedial program
reviewed, can counter the effect of these causes of underachievement and restore the child's ability to perform at an
expected level.

The reason for underachievement may also be the result of
an internal factor—genetics. This child may have physical
properties that set him off from the average or an inherent
inclination to follow paths that are not consistent with the
majority. The consequences of doing the natural thing for some
children is to separate themselves from the herd. Undirected,
the child with a difference may not learn to relate to the
existing world. In school and perhaps afterward, he is likely to
remain an underachiever. Parental guidance can be effective,
but only if provided with care, consideration, and flexibility.

The parent should attempt to determine the difference, if not
plainly obvious, in her child. Physical characteristics are
apparent to all. A girl may be prematurely developed, or much
too tall for the boys. A boy may be too short. Some children
adjust to such differences without difficulty.

In Part II, we surveyed some of the differences that might
cause underachievement. These may revolve around personality development, cognitive structures, and preferences. They
may be quite subtle. If there is a hint of a behavioral variation
in your child, you should ask questions based on your own
observations. Here are sample questions that can help get you
started:

- Is my child a loner? Does he have few or no friends? Does he prefer activities that require no one else? Is he disinterested in team sports and group games?
- Is my child an outside person? Do his chosen activities revolve around participant sports, fishing, swimming, camping, hiking, and trips? Is he always on the go? Is he weather-immune, not caring about the temperature or precipitation? Is he the natural personification of the post office slogan?
- Does my child show signs of becoming a night person? Is he especially difficult to wake up in the morning and equally troublesome to put to bed at night? Does he seem wide-awake when he should be sleeping, and sluggish when he should be fresh? Does he read under the covers with a flashlight or walk the halls when others are asleep? Does it seem impossible to tune his body clock?

Just as with intelligence, everyone has some of everything. A slight leaning or one incident doesn't make a child different. A consistent pattern does. If he's a nonconformist early, or if he demonstrates divergent thinking, or if he's just too bright, he may have a serious enough difference that can cause under-achievement. He may change on his own and, with time, become more like his peers, or he may remain different all of his life. Stan and Jerome are two classic examples of what may happen to this type of child.

"Different" should not be equated with failure. The child can learn to accept, live with, and use his differences to his advantage. Your job is to help. The underlying theme should be a recognition that the problem isn't necessarily the difference but the *attitude* engendered by the person with the difference.

Living with Realities

Talents in children, such as exceptional voice quality or athletic skills, are not likely to cause problems. In the same vein, being "different" does not necessarily imply that a problem exists. However, once the dissimilarity causes underperformance in school, it behooves the parent to render assistance.

Effective help must begin in the form of having the child understand that the difference actually exists. Parents should not sound the alarm, frighten a child, or in any way implant an unfavorable view that will impair the child's adjustment capabilities. The youngsters should be no more concerned than their friends who are left-handed. The difference may be an annoyance but certainly not life-shattering.

Take into account the nature and age of your child and his unique qualities. Help him to understand how:

- The majority of people usually think and act in given situations. The shortest boy in the class doesn't have to be told he's going to be first in line, but the divergent thinker must realize that some of his ideas may not be readily accepted. He should come to terms with the concept that others are not necessarily wrong but merely using mental procedures at variance with his own. He can then channel his abilities into forms that others will accept.

- Much of his success in school and elsewhere depends on his own attitude toward his difference. Some traits can be modified, such as a propensity for being late, but others will always remain. That little guy leading the line is not likely to become a professional basketball star but, just maybe, if he's so inclined and talented, he might become a pro jockey. That tall girl might some-day be a model and her short friend may learn to walk on extra high heels. Determine how the child feels. Stress the truth that physical, cultural, and ethnic differences are like book covers. Children and adults will be liked, appreciated, admired, or the opposite by their content, once it becomes known. Some basics will help your child gain acceptance by his peers. He should be led to understand that enthusiasm is contagious and dependability is an appreciated trait.

- The negative effects of differences, at times, can be overcome by some overt action on the part of the student. Some children can express their creative impulses, with parental encouragement, by forming clubs, "publishing" magazines, arranging trips and pursuing hobbies. As they get older, they may arrange vacations that satisfy their interests and find careers suitable to their natures. They automatically seek organizations of people with similar interests or peccadilloes.

- He can lead the best possible life by compromising his current desires in order to reap future rewards. A parent can teach an elementary school child the advantages of accepting delayed gratification. Parents can point out that virtually everything the child sees or uses involved a designer, architect, engineer, technician, and business manager. In his world, the child will need an education for any of these and related positions. Out of necessity, he will have to learn to work in harmony with others. To benefit from society's rules, he will have to follow them.

These explanations will probably be ongoing with increments of understanding. The different child will not put aside his penchant for doing things his own way but will learn how to live without conflict or with as little conflict as possible.

"It Might Have Been"

"You have to be ready and you have to pick the right time," explained Stanton. "The better your track record, the easier it gets. People start to listen.

"Your listeners have to understand your language and form a mental picture of your goal. They tend to resist anything new, involved, or confusing. You have to make your innovative ideas sound like a logical outgrowth of prior efforts by relating it to something familiar. Most of all, make it clear."

"Suppose they still don't understand?" asked Jerome.

"They might fight you or your idea. They won't admit any lack of comprehension but will usually refer to your position as muddled or impractical."

"What do you do then?"

"Prepare a better presentation," explained Stanton.

"Sounds too simple."

"It is simple. That's why it works. I might add a couple of suggestions. I don't usually give them everything at once and I anticipate their objections."

"Knowing you, you probably leave a door or two open so when they voice their disapproval, you can hit them with a barrage of sound arguments."

Stan smiled his confirmation.

"Aren't you being devious?" Jerome queried.

"No, just explaining how to get ideas approved. I do my homework, offer facts, and some original combinations of ideas. I make my plans as appetizing as I can and try hard for acceptance. Anyone who has better ideas can certainly offer them, but my efforts have made the company grow.

"We're not like most people, Jerome. I've learned to utilize that difference to the fullest and everyone benefits. The country is immersed in global competition. We're needed. Now. We were a great team as kids. Will you join me?"

Jerry effected his inimitable smile of encouragement, familiar to Stan in days long gone.

"All the way to Pennsylvania Avenue?"

"All the way."

Jerome sat with his eyes closed and visualized the combined meeting of the House and Senate. He saw Stan near the doorway adjusting his tie and tugging on his jacket. He didn't see himself. The speaker's voice boomed through the assembly. "Ladies and gentlemen, the President of the . . ."

An unsmiling Jerome stood. "Stan, I criticize others and then walk away. You act and accept responsibility for the results. I'm not prepared for what you're offering. Perhaps, if we had traveled the same road . . ."

Stan nodded. He, too, had sometimes felt the fear of failure but his drive for achievement was always stronger than his uncertainty. The former buddies shook hands.

Jerome started to smile again as he was exiting. "Maybe I'll send you a letter once in a while. Tell you what you're doing wrong."

Stan watched with regret as his childhood pal left the outer office. Perhaps he could think of something for Jerome later. He returned to his desk and pressed the intercom button.

"Liz. Bring your pad. There's work to do."

Wrap-Up

Intelligence alone is not a guarantee of achievement. Children must establish goals for themselves commensurate with their abilities. Children who are somewhat different need special goals that may depart from the mainstream.

Parental influence or lack of it may determine this type of child's future level of achievement—even through adulthood.

Assistance and some special effort on the parent's part are sometimes needed to acquire the desired attitude.

Differences may take many forms including personality variances, extremely high general or divergent intellect, or physiological characteristics.

There are few hermits today. Dissimilar or not, children must live in society as it exists. Sometimes they must adjust their way of thinking and persuade others to do the same in order to be accepted. For most, it is possible to retain and be comfortable with their uniqueness and still meet societal obligations.

A supercharged engine, preset at the factory, is no assurance of success. Parents must be involved with the driver to ensure proper handling of the power. Parents sometimes may be authoritarian; that is, give incontrovertible orders. At other times they may be democratic by involving the child in decision making. They should never be laissez-faire when the youngster is in his formative years. Jerome's parents held to a "hands-off" approach. Their involvement, at critical times, might have yielded favorable results.

Children who choose or must follow alternate highways may do very well if they recognize and accept some basic realities:

- The structure of society is based on the majority.
- They must, at times, censor their thoughts and rein in their activities.
- Most people have a bias against anything different.

- They must prepare and educate themselves to reach goals suitable for their own makeup.
- They must know when to compromise and when to yield. They must also recognize a favorable position and the right moment to prevail.

22

Parental Evaluations

Thinking in Class

What is Mrs. Carron saying? Oh, she's picking up where we stopped yesterday. Washington crossed the Delaware River to attack the Hessians. Why did he do that?

Why the Hessians? I thought he was fighting the British. Oh. She's explaining it. The Hessians were mercenaries. Soldiers who fought anyone for pay. The British had hired them. Why at Christmas? I know that. They wouldn't expect an attack then. They would be surprised.

Why did he attack at all? Here comes the answer. His troops needed a victory to build morale. Hey. That Washington was a good general. He understood people. Hold it! The teacher didn't say that. That's my thought. I'll just make a note here to remind me of it later.

Now. Where's the teacher going with this lesson? What is she telling us? Why?

Oh. That's what we have to do for homework. The details are in the book. We're to write about some part of it. Let's see. The numbers of soldiers on each side? Their weapons? Uniforms? The weather? No. Lots of kids will write that stuff. I wonder if I could write about how Washington understood people. The morale thing. If he built up the morale of his own men, wouldn't he be lowering the morale of the enemy? None of that seems to be in the book. I could go to the library and see what I can find out.

In a few moments, the child trained in employing skills can repeat the elements—once considered laborious—that are necessary to complete assignments. The child can identify major themes, the purposes of the lesson, and distinguish between these and interesting but superfluous information. The experienced learner deals with cause and effect, rather than extraneous matter. The reason why Washington attacked was the main idea; the uniforms of the respective armies was thrown in as an aside. The trained learner knows almost immediately what the teacher wants and where he can gather the desired information. His strategy, for the moment, is like freshly poured cement, but it will harden. He may, on reconsideration, modify his original thinking, but he already has a tentative plan of action. He has left a significant characteristic of underachievement behind. He has started. He is already thinking and planning. He has sketched out a goal and some possible ways to reach it.

You taught your child the fundamentals of doing assignments. Your goal was to convert basic steps into a habit—an automatic, timesaving, workable methodology of approaching a task. The boy in the illustration is demonstrating that he no longer has to call on a mental checklist of steps. He's concentrating on the job at hand. These steps take longer to climb initially, but soon become ingrained with repetition.

For instance, do you remember? Fasten seat belts. Check position of car gear. Place key into ignition. Turn key. Release key. Release emergency brake. Turn on lights, if needed. Check clearance before pulling out. Check mirrors for traffic. Depress gas pedal. Turn the wheel. Proceed with caution.

Your mind hasn't forgotten. The process has taken the elevator down into your subconscious. Every step is repeated every time you get into your automobile as the driver. Unless something is wrong, like the car not starting, you give it little conscious thought.

Taking Stock

Your remedial efforts should be producing results. An instantaneous turn around is quite possible, but not typical. You are more apt to get delayed positive reactions and gradual improvements. Work efforts may spike only to fall back again. You may see short periods of no advancement. In a general way, the progress of your child should resemble a somewhat bullish stock market. Periods of highs will be followed by drops but, in the aggregate, the learning curve will be rising.

Test scores and report card grades are good evaluative criteria for ascertaining the work of your child most of the time. Exceptions have been noted earlier. You might also develop a checklist to gauge progress and accomplishment that reveal additional information about your child. Choose those of the following that are appropriate for you and your child. Subjective or not, parents many times must use their own judgment in raising children. This is one of those times. The questions are based on the characteristics of an achiever and relate both to the emotional component of learning and his cognitive attack skills. A majority of affirmative answers is a very healthy sign.

Does your child now:

1. Start his assignments without undue prompting and avoid excuses for stalling or postponing?

2. Identify the reason for the work and the principal theme. Also, does he separate the details from the essence of the problem?

3. Understand what he is to do and how he is to do it before starting?

4. Develop a plan to reach identified goals and select the best tactics to employ?

5. Operate comfortably and effectively in his own learning style?

6. Avoid pitfalls that have bothered him before or rely on his experience to overcome these hurdles?

7. Work well with others when team efforts are required but also work well alone?

8. Listen to informed suggestions and try them out to determine if they work for him?

9. Seek assistance only after he has exhausted the other alternatives available to him?

10. Concentrate on the task he has started and show persistence in getting it done?

11. Evaluate his completed work in terms of what he set out to do?

12. Comprehend the meaning of the assignment and see how each component relates to this meaning?

13. Utilize his skills and knowledge in other assignments and in other activities?

14. Gauge his own progress on daily assignments, on his ongoing performance at school, and discount the possibility of any prolonged failure?

15. Satisfy himself that his work at home and in school is clear and accurate?

16. Feel confident that he can master any assignment and any test that he considers reasonable for his grade?

17. Rebound from difficult situations or setbacks with a determination that he will do better?

18. Display interest in a broad spectrum of subjects and activities and find new challenges exciting?

19. Give thought to these new situations and problems and attempt to dissect and analyze them?

20. Accept education as an important and integral part of his present and future life?

21. Accept the notion that some rewards are not immediate but are nevertheless worth earning?

22. Ask questions about news items, excursions taken, family history?

23. Show an interest in many areas unrelated to school?

24. Sometimes request explanations of adult behavior and decisions?

25. Try to solve difficult nonschool problems himself?

26. Refer to past adult remarks and statements and quote accurately?

27. Frequently initiate his own activities, make up games, and suggest them to others?

28. Share his experiences, pleasant or otherwise?

29. Display a developing sense of humor and laugh at himself at times?

Scoring

A multitude of intricate scoring systems for the questions could be devised, but none would enhance your child's academic career. They would probably be of little value and could even be misleading. Instead, use this simple device.

For each satisfactory answer record a "3." For each response that indicates some progress, place a "2." For the remainder, where performance is still inadequate, mark a "1."

Don't evaluate on the number of 3's, 2's, and 1's. That reveals little. Don't average, either. Your child could have half a dozen "1's" which are offset by half a dozen "3's." An average of those items masks the problem. The items with the "1" rating could be the cause of his underachievement. Although he may be strong in other areas, the high marks will not make up for his weak elements. He could be well adjusted socially but if he can't read well, he still has a problem.

The value of the system is to go beyond the numbers and locate the unacceptable areas. A "1" should be thought of as a red flag, a warning that something is wrong. A "2" should be colored yellow, a notice that progress is present but caution is indicated. A "3" simply means the question no longer pertains and may be disregarded.

Corrective Measures

Keeping records of progress may be helpful. You can compare today's evaluation with one completed a month earlier. In a question or two you may note a regression. This is to be expected. You're relying on a judgment call which may change slightly from day to day. You may have committed an error but don't get upset; professionals do too. Just make the correction. In addition, your child is not likely to perform at exactly the same level every minute. You only need an approximation. The purposes of the evaluation are to:

- Show your child how he has improved over time to reinforce his urge to succeed. The "3's" provide experience with success. Many parents have their young children stand against a doorjamb to mark their height. Physical growth comparisons can then be made. Comparative evaluations can provide growth data for academics and related areas.

- Help you determine any weakness that may be interfering with your attempts to raise your child's academic performance. You can congratulate yourself on the successful items but should focus on the ones failed.
- Identify problems that, in combination, may reveal areas of weakness that are not obvious when examined item by item.
- Save time by identifying attributes that require no special attention or reinforcement.
- Provide you with useful information to discuss with your child's teacher. If the two of you agree on a less-than-satisfactory characteristic, your efforts to remediate that item can be coordinated.
- Enable you to analyze your own thinking on a continuous basis to correct possible errors in guidance and approaches.

Playing Detective

Though all the pieces were in place, Doug's mother, Sheila, was still dissatisfied with his progress. Doug's grades had climbed over a four-month period. His teacher was favorably impressed with his recent efforts, and Doug himself seemed perfectly content. "How am I doing?" he asked frequently, quoting a former New York mayor. The child's father was also pleased and, annoyed at his wife's questioning, he chastised her. "You just expect too much from him. Let well enough alone."

"He has improved," she acknowledged, "but I just know he can do even better."

"It takes time. Now, why don't you pay more attention to some other things. Don't you think we're spending too much money on gifts?"

The unsure woman resented her husband's patronizing, but decided to avoid an issue. Doug was the problem, not petty squabbles. If her son was capable of better work, even though his current efforts had improved, and his grades were satisfactory, then he must still be an underachiever. That being the case, she reasoned, there is more remediation that must be applied. Back to the drawing board.

Sheila reviewed all the prescriptive sections of the program. I've done all that, she told herself. She rechecked her evaluative criteria. Seems fair, she commented silently. He doesn't rate "3's" for every question, but who does? As I understand it, it's the "1's" that point to trouble. No "1's."

It must be a matter of fine tuning, she decided. Doug's not weak anywhere but maybe not as strong as he might be.

The determined woman, with the help of her son, reviewed his recent homework notes. A test was forthcoming on Friday and Doug said he was already prepared. It was Wednesday. Using his notes, she asked questions. Doug answered each correctly. He knows the work, she concluded. I guess that's all I can do. Then she remembered the story of Adele's son.

She decided to prepare her own test based on the content of his homework and used the recommendations offered about testing. On Thursday evening, she told Doug, as part of his preparation for the upcoming examination, she wanted him to take a practice test. Doug was complacent; he saw nothing wrong with such an exercise.

Part 1 of the test Sheila constructed consisted of objective questions which Doug answered easily and confidently. He did not choke. So much for Adele's discovery. That's not it. Doug started part 2, an essay question. He proceeded to write without hesitation and continued until he was satisfied the work was complete. He then looked at his mother and grinned. "How am I doing?"

Sheila now felt a mixed feeling of success and concern. She had detected a flaw but first she must read his answer. She skipped the objective questions. The essay part confirmed her suspicion. Doug had, at least in part, missed the gist of the question, which was on the Civil War. He saw the word "slavery" and responded immediately to that. He understood the Northern and Southern disagreements on the slavery question and eagerly set about to record his knowledge. The question, however, was about states' rights. Doug, she realized, was an impulsive student. He fired before identifying his target.

"Just call me Sheila Holmes," she taunted her nonplussed

husband. "We should have known from his other activities. He always jumps before looking. Sometimes he hits test questions right but frequently doesn't. We can work on this."

As Sheila found out, there are an endless number of learning and performance problems. By reviewing the basics carefully, a parent may discover her own child's shortcoming, which is likely to be a variation of one of the fundamentals.

Follow the Rules?

Lori's weak area was well known to her parents and her teacher. The sixth-grader was active, bright, interested, and unprepared. She rarely did all of her homework and very often she did none.

"She'll soon be finding other interests and she's not doing her work now. What's going to happen when she has boys on her mind?"

"She may change. There's time. Let's be patient," her mother offered.

"She may change for the worse," admonished her father. "We just can't sit by and let her keep falling behind. Elementary school is the bedrock of education."

"I realize that. But what can we do about it? How can we change her?"

"Let's review that material again. Maybe we missed something," he said.

"She doesn't start as she should and she doesn't concentrate and she doesn't finish. That's clear," Lori's mother stated. "But, according to her teacher, she does those things all right in school."

"In school she's conforming. She's learned to do that. At home, what?" asked the concerned father.

"At home, she wants to break the rules. Maybe she doesn't think our rules are reasonable."

"Well, she's not going to break them," added her father.

"No. Wait a while. Maybe at home she wants to do her work her own way."

"Sure, with the radio blasting her off the chair. And how about the time she was insisting on watching that television special while she did her homework. Fat chance.''

"Hold on. We made her follow our rules.''

"Good common sense,'' said the father.

"Yes, and recommended by everyone. But remember that stuff about every child being unique and children using their own learning style?''

"Yes. Yes.'' answered the father. "But that doesn't mean mixing TV and radio with homework.''

"I wouldn't think so, either. But how far did we get doing it our way?''

"Nowhere.''

"Well?''

"Well, I don't think there's anything to lose.''

Lori was never told to do assignments her own way. She was told to do her homework. Period. The child spread out her work and moved things around. Both parents were in the next room watching television. They paid no attention to her. In a few minutes, she left. Neither parent objected. She then returned with her portable radio, turned on at low volume. The television watchers were silent. Lori looked furtively at them through the door and when they didn't return her glance, she turned the volume up.

The experiment was not an instant success. Lori's assignments were poorly done but showed gradual improvement. She then reached a point where the improvement accelerated. The child proved she could work with background music.

The rules governing learning seemed to clash in Lori's case, but they didn't. Concentration is necessary for efficient learning, but Lori and many others can focus their attention better with music than without. Just as liquid takes the shape of its container, learning conditions must be adapted to meet the needs of the learner.

Other Factors

If a child can do well and doesn't, an explanation for it lies somewhere. Parents may have to modify some of their remedial techniques. For instance, a child may be motivated, but not enough. The parent may have to upgrade the reward a bit. Increasing incentive has elicited better responses from many employees. It just may work for your child too. Sometimes a parent's expectations are too high, especially concerning the rate of the child's progress. Your child may not turn around immediately, but if you have deleted the impinging negatives and substituted the essentials of learning, you should see results.

There is an "unless"; in fact, there are two. One—parents usually point to the nullifying effect of peer pressure on their remedial program. Parents tend to blame "his friends" too readily but, in some cases, the wrong company may in fact be harmful. If there is substance to such a complaint, the parents obviously must make changes. Outside forces cannot be controlled by an educational program directed at the subject alone.

The other "unless" is the widely publicized classification known as learning disability, a minimal neurological impairment. You may not recognize a learning disability when you see it. The U.S. Office of Education defined the malady as a ". . . disorder in one or more of the basic psychological processes involved in understanding or in using language" and, because of this disorder, the child may demonstrate an "imperfect ability to listen, think, speak, read, write, spell, or do mathematical calculations." Dyslexia, thought to be a neurological problem that interferes with the ability to read, is an example of a learning disability. Sensory deficits and mental retardation were excluded from the definition. Thus, learning disabilities implies a short circuit in the child's neurological system that impedes normal learning. This condition, unclear and confusing, may not always be detected, especially when the degree of impairment is slight.

The chances are small that your child is affected, but sometimes, when improvement in scholarship tends to drag, parents become quite concerned. They may overemphasize any symptom and assume that their child is afflicted. The following common behavioral signs reported by parents are *not likely* indicators of a learning disability:

- A first-grader reverses the letters in words. This is a common maturational delay. By the time he's seven, this concern will probably be history.

- The child appears slow to understand concepts. How slow? He may not get away quickly at the starting gate, but if he catches up before he's overwhelmed with additional concepts, he doesn't have a problem. Fast learning is indeed associated with bright children, but there are many exceptions. Once he has grasped the idea, does he remember it and can he use it advantageously? If he can, there's no cause for alarm.
- Your first-grader demonstrates poor eye-hand coordination. This is likely another delayed maturational condition. Very common. Give him a few years.
- The child talks too much, as if driven. However, he stops when directed to do so. That's his personality, not neurological damage.
- The child resists going to school, finds excuses for staying home, says school is boring. He sounds like a perfectly normal underachiever.
- The child wants to play when he should be working and can't seem to comprehend the importance of school. He's probably just immature.
- The young student shows anxiety about taking tests or performing orally in school, but seems normal and natural at home. He may have had a negative school experience or may be extremely shy. Any one of these conditions lends itself to remediation.
- The youngster exhibits some speech problems, such as difficulty in pronouncing the "th" sound. Most of these are functional and will fade away with time or can be treated effectively by speech therapists.
- Your child performs well below his expected level without a detectable explanation. Neither encouragement nor punishment has been beneficial. He's probably an underachiever and not learning disabled. Recheck the causes of underperformance. Consider possible variations.
- Sometimes your child works well and at other times he does not. His performance-swings seem unrelated to any particular event. This does not sound like a learning disability.

Some of the symptoms attributed to learning disabilities are merely a lack of readiness in young children. Educators know that youngsters mature at different rates. Many pupils in the primary grades, for instance, have difficulty using fine motor skills. They shouldn't be labeled, treated, or rushed. They're perfectly normal children with their own personal growth calendars.

Many children have minor, correctable problems that disappear with time and routine remediation. Learning disabilities, to many of us, refer to severe disabling characteristics that usually include emotional problems. A small sampling of indications of learning disabilities and/or emotional disturbances follow. Even these may be attributable to various other causes but, if present, require a professional diagnosis.

The child is:

- Erratic—shows inconsistent behavior in similar situations
- Always blames someone else for his failure or for something he did but shouldn't have
- Quarrelsome, belligerent, impudent, tantrum-prone, frustrated, oversensitive
- Profoundly immature
- Easily distracted, inattentive
- Reversing letters at seven years of age or older
- Showing difficulty in reproducing information by writing or drawing
- Confused over figure-background relationships (trouble separating an object from the background)
- Confusing his left and his right, and has an extremely poor sense of direction
- Confusing words of similar sounds
- Awkward, has difficulty in drawing circles, throwing, catching, and pointing to his body parts

Too many children are irresponsibly assigned to learning-disabled classes when, in reality, they are "only underachievers." Symptoms may appear to overlap but there is a critical difference between them. Learning-disabled children suffer from some known or unknown neurological debilitation. Underachieving children are reacting to unique urges, unfavorable experiences, or unsatisfactory environments. The difference, therefore, should be traced back to *why* they don't perform at their innate ability level. Learning-disabled children can't; underachieving children don't want to.

Wrap-Up

Underachieving children respond to remedial programs at different rates. Just changing a faulty spark-plug may make a missing engine run perfectly. One corrective aspect of the program may bring about a similar response in your child. However, some children require a complete learning overhaul.

When a child's school grades climb to an acceptable level, the parent should adopt a consultant's role. The parent who has become a crutch should back off gradually. The child must learn to walk without assistance.

If the child's improvement is not yet satisfactory, the parent should evaluate the youngster's achievement in the various areas recommended. Those aspects that appear weakest should then be reinforced.

Children should be involved in evaluating their own work record. Very often the child himself will provide the key to the solution of difficulties.

While the program enumerates many causes that go beyond the typical "He's lazy" theory, they are not all-inclusive. Some variation of these causes may slow progress.

If learning disabilities are suspected, examinations should be performed by a learning disability specialist, a psychologist experienced in the field, and a competent neurologist.

Learning-disabled children are in state and federally recognized financially supported programs. Underachievers, on the other hand, are so numerous that school districts couldn't afford to create classes just for them. Parents must therefore utilize their own remedial program and work with the child's teachers to bring about desired change.

23

Final Wrap-Up

PARENT: According to the remedial program the first step is to
determine if my child is an underachiever. Suppose he isn't
"substantially below his potential?" He doesn't meet your
definition. But still, he's not working up to his best level.
Can't the program help?

THERAPIST: Everything in the program is an educational procedure. There are many considerations, but I suspect that future
curricula for all normal children will be very similar.
Therefore, use any aspect that might help the child.

PARENT: Why the sense of humor requirement?

THERAPIST: Sometimes, it's contagious. Everyone falls down.
Your child isn't a machine. You want him to laugh at
situations and at himself. The program is serious only in
terms of its goals. The implementation part is games and fun.

PARENT: The parental time involved could be a problem,
couldn't it?

THERAPIST: It could but shouldn't be. Your kid deserves some of
your attention; some moments that are not perfunctory. You
can sit down and ask "What shall we talk about?" if he has
something to say. But if you just sit and look at each other,
you're wasting time.

   If he's in the program, he'll have a great deal to report and
discuss. He'll be looking forward to sharing his experiences

about school, neighborhood activities, his hobbies, his friends, his homework.

PARENT: My son will always give me fits about doing homework.

THERAPIST: No. I don't agree. Many children will start out that way because homework appears irrelevant, too difficult, or a squandering of their free time.

Homework can be a game if they see a reason for doing it, know how to get it done accurately, and earn a feeling of success.

A little reward here and there helps too.

PARENT: I can see that some planning will provide the efficiency I need to do my end of the program. But you recommend all those excursions to develop curiosity and interest. I can do some, but not all of them.

THERAPIST: You're not going to do everything I've outlined right away. You can do some of the things over time. You should also get all the help available.

PARENT: Help? What help? I get virtually none.

THERAPIST: Create some.

PARENT: How?

Busy Parents

"I don't have time for all those recommended trips. I work a full week and when I'm off, I still have cleaning and laundry and shopping. Just how am I supposed to do all of this?"

The problem of too many time-consuming commitments has increased for parents over the past 15 years. Parental obligations to children are not negated or lessened by other demands on their time. Parents must use some initiative in finding solutions to problems created by the requirements of their work.

The obvious remedies are not always possible. You can hire someone for housekeeping but you must be able to afford it. You can have your own parents fill in for you but they are not always available, able, or willing. Many grandparents still help but others feel they've already raised their own families and now prefer time to themselves.

As a parent, you should try for all the assistance you can

afford or inveigle, but most of the time this is not enough. Use, then, whatever is possible. You may have to be somewhat enterprising, but there are ways.

- If there are older siblings, have them escort their younger brothers and sisters when necessary.
- Utilize the services of high school students who, after school or Saturdays, can take your child to a planned event. The baby-sitter can be an escort.
- Create trip pools with other parents. In some situations, car pools can be effective with individuals taking turns doing the driving. The same concept may be applicable to excursions. Team up with another parent or two to alternate escorting your respective youngsters for learning experiences. One parent takes her own and two others while the other two parents attend to other matters.
- Use only part of the day for a short trip. You need not go everywhere or require a long day each time. Frequently, a few hours will suffice. Plan in accordance with your other obligations.
- Search for outings sponsored by neighborhood organizations and churches. For relatively small fees, many clubs arrange supervised bus trips to places of interest. If you can't find any, or there are not enough, organize your own. Take the lead in forming excursion clubs for children. Insist that any parent who wants her child included do some important phase of the work or lead the next trip.
- Suggest to your neighborhood principal that trips be part of the after-school activities. More and more post-school day programs are being designed by school administrators and parents. Taxpayers are already paying for the buildings and buses. Both should be utilized more extensively. The increased costs for the activities mentioned are not substantial. School districts, more than ever, desire the good will of parents. Give them some ideas and give them your support.

Parents are often surprised at how much can be done if they try. Many others are in precisely your position—time-strapped and without surplus funds. By joining in a common effort with other adults, you can provide much for your child that is not presently available.

Cooperative efforts inspire more than curiosity and motivational development by means of tours. Leave yourself open to suggestions from others. Even ideas that have misfired for other groups may be helpful to yours.

A mother listened as her friend reported an experiment that failed.

"We thought we could have our two children do their homework together. Both of our kids weren't doing as well as they could. So we arranged to alternate houses Monday through Thursday. Anyhow, the kids loved the idea, but it didn't work. They just told each other stories, and giggled and did very little work. We tried standing over them but still nothing got done. We gave it up."

The listening parent liked the concept anyway, and called a neighbor whose child was one year older than hers. Neither child was failing, but they weren't reaching their potentials either. After some discussion, they decided on a modification of the original plan.

The two children took turns going to each other's houses at a prescribed time. The "sending mother" stayed home while the "host" parent supervised the children.

The result was a pleasant surprise for both parents. Each child not only completed the assignment but no longer resented doing homework.

"We were just lucky, I guess. We had the right combination. My Helen was a year older than Tyler and things just fell into place.

"We didn't have any of that joking around. Helen adopted the role of a teacher and helped Tyler understand his work, which was easy for her. She seemed to understand any material that perplexed him. She explained things in ways he understood.

"Then she became very serious about her own work as she showed Tyler how a 'more mature' student acts. She was playing out her role, I guess, but I certainly wasn't arguing with the results.

"As for Tyler, he now had someone who 'understood' his

problems, was right there when he needed her, and gave him some very special attention.

"My friend and I felt the satisfaction of helping our children and every other day we had free time we could use for other purposes."

Another parent paid an older child a comparatively small amount to act as a tutor for her child. The parent, on a weekly basis, set up objectives for her child based on the remedial program and the school's study unit. She reviewed these with her paid helper, who spent four hours a week with her child.

Sometimes another child can communicate with a peer when an adult can't, or loses patience, or simply hasn't adequate time. Utilize the services of other children on occasion to repair the cracks in your program.

Help may come from unexpected sources. Eric was one of those classic underachievers who found school very distasteful. Five days in a row of schooling was his maximum. His mother felt the weekend should be enough for him to "recover" from his "ordeal," but the second-grader felt differently. School made him physically ill. His mother said that was not possible, but he knew better. After a long week in the classroom, he was given temporary relief by Saturday and Sunday. But then came Monday. He personally was willing to attend school, but his body refused. Mom just didn't realize how bad it was. Sure. He didn't have a fever but he was dizzy and felt like throwing up. He would report this to the teacher who would send him to the nurse. The nurse then would call Mom at work and Mom would say he was all right. The nurse would let him lie on the cot for a few minutes and then send him back to class. And, according to Eric, he was really sick.

Eric's mother spoke to the child's pediatrician during an office visit.

"I really didn't know what else to do, doctor. I don't see signs of anything and the fact that this 'illness' occurs on Mondays and after holidays is too much of a coincidence. What do you think?"

"I think it's clear enough. Eric gets himself all worked up over going to school and does feel those symptoms he complains of. Let me talk to him alone."

The worried parent waited while her son and the

physician held their conference behind closed doors. In a few minutes, the door opened and a happy-faced seven-year-old came out.

"Okay, Mom. Let's go."

The parent looked at the pediatrician, who responded with a nod. "I think we just may have a solution."

Eric, holding something in his hand, had some difficulty putting on his coat.

"What's that, dear?"

"It's my card. I mean the doctor's card."

"His card?"

"That's right. It has Dr. Lear's name and phone number on it."

"And?"

"He said any time I get sick in school, I'm to call him right at his office. He wrote something for the school nurse on the back. See? She's to let me use her phone."

Eric never made the phone call, but he knew he could if he wanted to. The Monday symptoms vanished and at some time before the end of the year the card was misplaced. Eric, at this stage, was still an underachiever, but he wasn't a sick one. His mother was no longer bothered by the nurse's phone calls nor Eric's morning protestations.

Technology

PARENT: Technology today encompasses everything. Other than your recommendation to use audio tapes and television for news programs, you have avoided the subject.

THERAPIST: I haven't avoided it. I've just excluded it. I consider the modern electronic devices an essential part of everyday life and that includes the classroom. As sound, effective systems become available, schools should utilize them.

PARENT: What about in the home?

THERAPIST: Use anything that seems to help but be cautious. A parent should not employ any system that impedes the efforts of the school. One of the main themes of the program is to work with the school, not in opposition to it. The instruction in the classroom and at home should blend.

PARENT: Don't computers help children to learn?

THERAPIST: Yes, they offer definite advantages. Any youngster starting school today should be thoroughly familiar with computers by the time he graduates from high school and perhaps before that.

However, there is a caveat. The underachieving child, already lacking in self-esteem or suffering the consequences of poor experiences, may be facing a challenge too difficult for him at the time. The negative aspects of his makeup may be reinforced. Technology, yes, but only as he is ready for it.

PARENT: For other children, the light is green for computers?

THERAPIST: Yes, but . . .

PARENT: Another caution?

THERAPIST: Yes. There is a tendency for people to want fast and simple solutions. Phonics. Back to basics. Mainstreaming. More money. Higher standards. There is no "quick fix."

Technology is not the panacea for all of our learning problems. It has a definite and integral role in education but is still and will continue to be only one segment out of many paths. Let's be prudent.

Screening

PARENT: You contend that parents are not responsible if their children become underachievers, but they share the blame if their children continue to be.

THERAPIST: In general, that statement is true, but certainly not one hundred percent of the time. There are just too many possible exceptions to make it a rule.

PARENT: What else, if anything, should a parent do?

THERAPIST: I would use the term "urge." Parents of children who are underachievers, or even borderline underachievers, should have their youngsters checked medically.

PARENT: You mean beyond treatment for illness and routine checkups?

THERAPIST: Exactly. Medical problems, not usually detectable by laypeople, may curtail learning. For instance, Colin was in the second grade when an astute teacher noticed something wrong. Sometimes the boy would not respond when called on. He would just sit there and ignore her. Most of the time, he joined the lesson with some enthusiasm and made a very satisfactory contribution.

"He does that at home, too," his mother explained to the teacher. "I guess he just gets moody or stubborn."

The parts of the puzzle don't fit, the teacher thought. Perhaps Colin was a daydreamer and, alone with his thoughts, just didn't hear himself being addressed. Gestalt! Insight! That must be it, thought the teacher, suddenly excited. He didn't hear. Not because his mind was elsewhere. He actually didn't hear the sound of the words at times. It could be an auditory problem.

The teacher made a point of moving about the class and started to call on Colin from different locations in the room. Colin responded. Then, one time, as the children were working on a drawing, standing to Colin's right and slightly behind him, she called his name softly. No response.

She moved to his left and again softly said, "Colin." The child turned toward her and said "Yes?" Later, the audiologist reported a hearing deficit in Colin's right ear.

Visual problems of various kinds may not be noticed by parents or teachers either. Young children don't know what they're supposed to see and may not report a distortion.

PARENT: My child's school examines all of the children. They told me they'll pick up anything wrong ninety-five percent of the time.

THERAPIST: They'll notice anything of major import. It's these slight flaws that may get by.

PARENT: But ninety-five percent?

THERAPIST: The odds aren't good enough. If ninety-five percent of sensory problems are found we can assume that five percent are not. Is that cause for alarm? It is, if *your* child is one that is missed.

You want to eliminate any factor contributing to your child's underachievement. Discuss possible medical reasons with your family physician and let him either test your child or send him to specialists.

PARENT: Okay. Don't discount anything. Be sure.

THERAPIST: Right. Remember that technology is also advanced in medicine. Where your child is concerned, be sure nothing is medically wrong.

Critical Thinking

"A certain percentage of children have the habit of thinking; one of the aims of education is to break this habit."—Bertrand Russell.

PARENT: Some people are now saying the schools should do more about teaching children how to think. If my son is an underachiever now, how is he ever going to handle that?

THERAPIST: I don't see a problem. The basis for analytical thinking is built into the prescriptive curriculum starting with doing homework. It's in the foundation and columns of the remedial structure. The child is learning to determine what a topic or assignment is all about. He is asking "why." He's not just learning that George Washington crossed the Delaware to attack the enemy. He should also be asking what was his purpose?

From the beginning of this remedial program, the child is directed toward decision making after he collects the facts. His skill development in this area is not divorced from but rather incorporated into his regular school. It's anchored in a concrete subject, not in abstractions. He has to learn how to think in order to carry out the plan. While he's mastering this skill, he's also learning to apply this thinking to later subjects and to the world. He's learned to identify problems not plainly obvious and to search for many possible solutions. He's asking "What if" questions that require him to build conclusions based on actual data. The program, through incremental steps and practice, teaches him to draw inferences from given facts.

PARENT: Then he has the edge on his peers?

THERAPIST: I think he has on many of them. He has the requirements for reflective judgment.

PARENT: Forget the memorization.

THERAPIST: No. Again, the mistake in education is using the either/or principle. Some things should be learned by rote.

PARENT: Like what?

THERAPIST: The alphabet. There is no logical reason for the order of the letters but that's the way much of our information is arranged, from dictionaries to telephone directories.

PARENT: What else?

THERAPIST: The multiplication table. He can work this out logically but the time involved will interfere with other calculations. He should memorize it. He should know that seven times eight is fifty-six without doubt or hesitation.

PARENT: So some basics are still valuable.

THERAPIST: Yes. Rote learning has a limited but essential role.

Your child should master both arms of learning: the cognitive and the affective. Once he has learned how to learn in changing circumstances and how to transfer his skill and knowledge to new challenges, he will be an achiever. And more.

INDEX